The Book of Isaiah

OneBook.

DAILY-WEEKLY

The Book of Isaiah

Chapters 40–55

John Oswalt

 Seedbed

Cover design by Strange Last Name
Page design by PerfecType

Oswalt, John.

The Book of Isaiah : chapters 40-55 / John Oswalt. – Frankin, Tennessee : Seedbed Publishing, ©2016.

x, 181 pages ; 21 cm. + 1 videodisc – (OneBook. Daily-weekly)

ISBN 9781628243499 (paperback)
ISBN 9781628243536 (DVD)
ISBN 9781628243505 (Mobi)
ISBN 9781628243512 (ePub)
ISBN 9781628243529 (uPDF)

1. Bible. Isaiah, XL-LV -- Textbooks. 2. Bible. Isaiah, XL-LV -- Study and teaching.
3. Bible. Isaiah, XL-LV -- Commentaries.   I. Title. II. Series.

BS1520 .O88 2016   224/.106   2016949737

SEEDBED PUBLISHING
Franklin, Tennessee
Seedbed.com

CONTENTS

CONTENTS

CONTENTS

CONTENTS

WELCOME TO THE ONEBOOK: DAILY-WEEKLY

John Wesley, in a letter to one of his leaders, penned the following,

> O begin! Fix some part of every day for private exercises. You may acquire the taste which you have not: what is tedious at first, will afterwards be pleasant.
>
> Whether you like it or not, read and pray daily. It is for your life; there is no other way; else you will be a trifler all your days. . . . Do justice to your own soul; give it time and means to grow. Do not starve yourself any longer. Take up your cross and be a Christian altogether.

Rarely are our lives most shaped by our biggest ambitions and highest aspirations. Rather, our lives are most shaped, for better or for worse, by those small things we do every single day.

At Seedbed, our biggest ambition and highest aspiration is to resource the followers of Jesus to become lovers and doers of the Word of God every single day; to become people of One Book.

To that end, we have created the OneBook: Daily-Weekly. First, it's important to understand what this is not: warm and fuzzy sentimental devotions. If you engage the Daily-Weekly for any length of time, you will learn the Word of God. You will grow profoundly in your love for God, and you will become a passionate lover of people.

How does the Daily-Weekly work?

Daily. As the name implies, every day invites a short but substantive engagement with the Bible. Five days a week you will read a passage of Scripture followed by a short segment of teaching and closing with questions for reflection and self-examination. On the sixth day, you will review and reflect on the prior five days.

Weekly. Each week, on the seventh day, find a way to gather with at least one other person doing the study. Pursue the weekly guidance for gathering.

Share learning, insight, encouragement, and most important, how the Holy Spirit is working in your lives.

That's it. When the twelve weeks are done we will be ready with twelve more. Four times a year we will release a new edition of the Daily-Weekly. Over time, those who pursue this course of learning will develop a rich library of Bible learning resources for the long haul. Following is the plan for how we will work our way through the Bible.

The Gospels: Twelve weeks of the year the Daily-Weekly will delve into one of the Gospels, either in a broad overview or through a deep-dive into a more focused segment of the text.

The Epistles: Twelve weeks of the year the Daily-Weekly will explore one of the letters, sermons, or the Acts of the Apostles that make up the rest of the New Testament.

The Wisdom Writings: Twelve weeks of the year the Daily-Weekly will lead us into some part of the Psalms, Proverbs, or prophetic writings.

The Old Testament: Twelve weeks of the year the Daily-Weekly will engage with some portion of the Books of Moses (Genesis–Deuteronomy), the historical books, or other writings from the Old Testament.

If you are looking for a substantive study to learn Scripture through a steadfast method, look no further.

WEEK ONE

Isaiah 40:1–5, 8–14, 18–31

The Incomparable God

INTRODUCTION

The Judean people had lost everything. They had lost their country, their homes, many of their family members, their livelihoods—but even more, their hope. They had been sure that they were the chosen people of Yahweh, who was the sole God of the universe. They had been certain that he would protect them from the pagan Babylonians, who worshiped false gods, gods made with human hands. Surely, they thought, he would not allow his holy city and temple to be destroyed by people like that.

But now the unthinkable had happened. The Babylonians had captured all the land, and after a siege extending over two and a half years, had captured Jerusalem itself, desecrating the temple and destroying the city that had dared to rebel against them. Then they took the leadership of the nation into exile in Babylon, leaving only the poor and helpless behind.

But as bad as all that was, the worst thing was the almost inescapable conclusion that all their religious convictions had been wrong. Apparently they were *not* the chosen people; apparently Yahweh was *not* the sole god of the universe; evidently he was not even strong enough to defeat the Babylonian gods. All the promises that had shaped their lives were apparently false. How do you go on living when there is nothing left to live for?

To be sure, if the Judean people had listened to their prophets, they would have had a better understanding of what was happening. These recent events had not been a contest between Yahweh and the pagan gods, but were an example of Yahweh's ability to use even pagan nations to discipline his people. Indeed, the Judeans were his chosen people, but that did not, as they thought, give them a "pass" to live any way they chose and still be guaranteed security, comfort, and pleasure. In fact, precisely because he had chosen them and entered into an exclusive covenant with them, the expectations were all the higher. What happened to them was the result of nearly a thousand years of breaking their covenant over and over until even the patience of God was worn out.

So what does Yahweh say to these discouraged, disillusioned, defeated, sinful people? Is he done with them? Has he given up on them? If he is not defeated by the Babylonians, is he defeated by the Judeans' persistent sinning? This chapter answers these questions with a resounding, "No." God's love for them has not changed; his power over all creation is not diminished, and his intention to deliver them is forever the same. He *wants* to deliver, he *can* deliver, and he *will* deliver. He says the same to you and me. Whatever the bondage in which we may find ourselves, this delivering word is for us.

ONE

Does He Care about You?

Isaiah 40:1–5 *Comfort, O comfort my people, says your God. ²Speak tenderly to Jerusalem, and cry to her that she has served her term, that her penalty is paid, that she has received from the LORD's hand double for all her sins.*

³A voice cries out: "In the wilderness prepare the way of the LORD, make straight in the desert a highway for our God. ⁴Every valley shall be lifted up, and every mountain and hill be made low; the uneven ground shall become level, and the rough places a plain. ⁵Then the glory of the LORD shall be revealed, and all people shall see it together, for the mouth of the LORD has spoken."

Understanding the Word. Suppose you were given the responsibility of speaking to someone who had persistently hurt you, had broken every promise he or she had made to you, had borrowed a great deal of money from you and had never paid back a cent, and on top of it all, had slandered you repeatedly to other people. Now that person is in prison for having done those same things to a lot of other people, and you are supposed to go and talk with him or her. What will you say?

2

I think I might say something like, "Well, I hope you have learned your lesson. You have gotten exactly what you deserved, and you need to use your time in here to straighten up. Stop pitying yourself, and face up to what kind of a person you have made of yourself." Would you say something like that too?

That was the situation God was facing with his people. They were experiencing the results of many years of persistently doing exactly what their sworn covenant with Yahweh had told them not to do. They had sworn in blood (Exod. 24:6–8) that they *would* do what reflected his character and would *not* do what did not reflect his character. Then they had turned right around and done the opposites.

In the light of all that, what God says to them (and us) is shocking. He says, "Don't be discouraged! Don't give up. I am going to come and help you!" This is the meaning of the Hebrew word that is translated "comfort." It means to encourage, to strengthen, to stiffen. God takes no comfort when we are discouraged and depressed over our sins and failures. He does not say, "Well, good for you. I'm glad you finally got what you deserved." No, although we may have richly deserved what has happened to us ("received . . . double for all her sins," Isa. 40:2), he does not enjoy our ruin the way a vengeful human would. If he has brought us down, it is for the sole purpose of raising us back up.

How will he raise us up? He himself will come to us. He is so eager to do that that he calls for building a superhighway so that nothing will impede him (Isa. 40:2–3). All through the Scripture, the good news is that God is with us (see Genesis 39:2, 23). Yes, he is the transcendent one, who is utterly other than we are. Yet he enters into our lives and shares himself intimately with us. But is that just a metaphor, a figure of speech? No, it has become a fact. And the New Testament's use of these words tells us how the promise has become a fact (Matt. 3:3; Mark 1:2–3; Luke 3:4–6). Jesus Christ is the living evidence of God's love toward us. In spite of our claims to self-sufficiency; in spite of our trying to be God, to take his place in our lives; in spite of all the sins we have committed, God has come to us in Jesus Christ. He is *with* us in the truest sense of that word. He knows what it is to be confined within with human limitations. He knows what it is to be tempted almost beyond endurance. He knows what it is to be pressed and harassed with all the cares of life. But most of all, by becoming one of us, while still being God, he has been able to take all our guilt and condemnation upon himself. So whatever you are facing today,

God says, "Don't give up. Give it to me and let me carry it, and carry it away." He, who is the full manifestation of the glory of God (John 1:14; Col. 2:9), has come to be with us.

1. What is the most discouraging thing you are facing in your life today? What will it take for you to give that over to God?

2. What encouraging word would God like to speak to you today?

3. What roadblock is standing in the middle of God's superhighway into your heart today?

TWO

The Word, the Mighty Arm of God

Isaiah 40:8–11 *The grass withers, the flower fades; but the word of our God will stand forever. ⁹Get you up to a high mountain, O Zion, herald of good tidings; lift up your voice with strength, O Jerusalem, herald of good tidings, lift it up, do not fear; say to the cities of Judah, "Here is your God!" ¹⁰See, the Lord GOD comes with might, and his arm rules for him; his reward is with him, and his recompense before him. ¹¹He will feed his flock like a shepherd; he will gather the lambs in his arms, and carry them in his bosom, and gently lead the mother sheep.*

Understanding the Word. God had promised to come to his people and deliver them from the consequences of their sin. Those consequences were twofold: captivity in Babylon and alienation from God. But the questions remained: Could he do that, and how would he do it? For the fact is, human power and obstinacy can often seem almost inseparable. Perhaps you have encountered some of this in your own life, both in others and in yourself. We are in some unhealthy relationship, and there seems no way out. Someone is in a position of authority over you, and it seems as if he or she "has it in for you." You have tried to make some positive changes in your own behaviors and attitudes, and it has just seemed to come to nothing. What can God do about these kinds of things? Religious hope is a fine thing, but sometimes we just have to face reality, don't we?

4

The Judeans certainly felt this. After all, God hadn't seemed able to do anything to protect his city and land from the tyrant Nebuchadnezzar. And as for themselves, God didn't seem to have been able to produce any real changes in them in the previous millennium or so. Human power and obstinacy seem like pretty enduring things.

But Yahweh's response was very direct and forthright. He said human beings are to him nothing more than a field of blowing grass. Grass comes up in a great hurry and produces pretty little flowers, and a whole field of it seems very impressive. But it takes nothing more than a hot wind (and in Israel, they knew about hot winds) to dry up that whole field in a matter of hours.

For us humans, God's word is that hot wind. That is an interesting point. It is not that we humans are grass compared to God, but we are grass compared to God's word. Why does Isaiah say it like that? I think "word" here has three connotations. First, it speaks of God's power to command. All the Creator has to do to make something happen in his creation is to speak the word. The Roman centurion recognized that Jesus had power like that (Luke 7:6–8; see also Isaiah 11:4; 49:1). The second connotation is the absolute reliability of God's promises. If he says something will happen, you *know* it will happen. But there is an even deeper significance here. Yahweh is, above everything else, the God who speaks. He is the God who communicates. So it is no accident at all that Jesus is called "the Word" (see John 1:1, 14). Jesus is the final communication of the Creator's unchanging promise to save the world (1 Peter 1:24–25). No human will ever stand against the Word of God. What we can do is climb the highest mountain and shout to the world, "God's Word has come!"

But there is another image that appears in this passage. That is "the arm" of God (Isa. 40:10). This is especially a symbol of God's strength to accomplish his purpose. That thought is very clear here. God is coming, and he is going to reward some and pay back others. His mighty arm is going to strike out and deliver his people, no matter what the Babylonians think or plan. He is going to pick his people up out of the dust they have so richly deserved and seat them on thrones.

But the final verse in today's passage portrays another side to God's mighty arm. Here we see that twenty-seven-inch bicep being a pillow for a sleeping lamb, while with his other great arm, he gently leads the mother. Our God is mighty enough to deliver us from any human enemy and tender enough to restore us to himself from our deepest sins. All flesh is grass, but God's word is forever, and his arm can deliver us from anything.

1. What "enemy" holds you captive today? What does God say about it?

2. What is the right perspective on your situation? What can you do to maintain that perspective?

3. What are some ways in which God's mighty arm has been displayed in your life?

THREE

The Incomparable God

Isaiah 40:12–14, 18–20 *Who has measured the waters in the hollow of his hand and marked off the heavens with a span, enclosed the dust of the earth in a measure, and weighed the mountains in scales and the hills in a balance? [13] Who has directed the spirit of the* Lord, *or as his counselor has instructed him? [14] Whom did he consult for his enlightenment, and who taught him the path of justice? Who taught him knowledge, and showed him the way of understanding? . . .*

[18] To whom then will you liken God, or what likeness compare with him? [19] An idol?—A workman casts it, and a goldsmith overlays it with gold, and casts for it silver chains. [20] As a gift one chooses mulberry wood—wood that will not rot— then seeks out a skilled artisan to set up an image that will not topple.

Understanding the Word. The first eleven verses of this chapter spoke of God's desire and power to save his people from their captivity. But we can hear the Judean captives saying, "That is all well and good. But what about the Babylonian gods? They are not just going to stand by and let Yahweh take their slaves away." So the question is: How is it that God can actually make good on his promises? This is a very important issue, but a somewhat complex one, so stick with me here.

Why have people constructed gods, not only physical idols, but also the concepts behind the idols? The answer is fairly simple. We want to control the forces of the cosmos, whether they be psychic, social, or physical, for our own benefit. So around the world people have imagined these forces as humans;

we have made them in our image, as it were. We have done this because we think we know how to control humans. But for purposes of control, it is necessary that there be no boundaries between the human, the natural, and the divine. This way, what I as a human do here will automatically be duplicated in the divine realm, and that will be duplicated in the natural realm. The idol is the perfect expression of this: it is a natural object in human form that is an expression of the divine. So I want rain? I do a ritual that perhaps involves pouring out water on the idol. That means that the god pours out water in heaven, which means that the heavens pour water on the earth.

But if the gods are just humanized cosmic powers (rain, sun, moon, storm, passion, fertility, etc.), where did they come from and what is the purpose of it all? There is, of course, no answer. There are complicated stories about how the gods emerged sexually from the watery chaos that has always existed, and then took counsel among themselves how to destroy chaos and make order, but none of that explains why we are here, and for what reason we exist. Just as the sun knows no answer to such questions as these, neither does the sun god.

It is over against that understanding of reality, the one that permeated the whole ancient world all the way up to Rome, that Isaiah is writing. He reflects a completely opposite understanding of reality, the one that totally permeates the Bible. Yahweh, I AM, is a divine person who exists outside of the cosmos. He made the world by himself on purpose. He made it to be a home for persons like himself, whom he could bless in a life-giving relationship with himself. In short, he made us to share his character and his life. So where is the hitch? The hitch is that he is not the world and cannot be manipulated through the world. We cannot make him do what we want. We can only surrender our needs and ourselves to him, trusting that he knows our needs better than we do and that all his purposes toward us are good. Scary!

But that is exactly what Isaiah is saying. No human has made God in our image. He is the only God, and there is no other. He is not one of the forces of this world, with a human mask on. He didn't have a conference with some other gods to figure out how to destroy chaos. He made this world with a great and blessed purpose. We *can* trust him, if we will. But we must be forever careful of thinking that we can manipulate him to supply our needs. To do that is to reduce him to an idol, a god we have made so that we can control our world. Yahweh is a God unlike any of the human creations that we call gods.

He had the power to create the world from nothing, and he has the power to deliver us.

1. What are some ways that we think we can manipulate God through our actions?

2. The apostle Paul says that covetousness (greed) is idolatry (Col. 3:5; Eph. 5:5). Why do you think he says that?

3. Washing my car on Sunday does not mean the car is my idol. But when can the car, or anything else, become an idol for me?

FOUR

Who Is My Equal?

Isaiah 40:21–26 *Have you not known? Have you not heard? Has it not been told you from the beginning? Have you not understood from the foundations of the earth? 22It is he who sits above the circle of the earth, and its inhabitants are like grasshoppers; who stretches out the heavens like a curtain, and spreads them like a tent to live in; 23who brings princes to naught, and makes the rulers of the earth as nothing.*

24Scarcely are they planted, scarcely sown, scarcely has their stem taken root in the earth, when he blows upon them, and they wither, and the tempest carries them off like stubble.

25To whom then will you compare me, or who is my equal? says the Holy One. 26Lift up your eyes on high and see: Who created these? He who brings out their host and numbers them, calling them all by name; because he is great in strength, mighty in power, not one is missing.

Understanding the Word. In these verses Isaiah continues his argument that there is no other power in the cosmos that can prevent Yahweh from accomplishing the deliverance that he promises. Here he underlines Yahweh's absolute uniqueness, the point that he began to make in verse 12 and following. The technical term for this uniqueness is *transcendence*. This is the idea that God is absolutely other than his creation. It did not somehow emerge from his body; it is not a manifestation of his essence; he is outside of it and beyond it.

This is the true significance of the term that is a particular favorite of Isaiah's: "the Holy One" (v. 25). To be holy in essence is to be somehow out of the ordinary. But the Old Testament writers declare that none of the gods has a right to be called holy. A block of wood carved to look like a man . . . holy? Of course not! Human passion conceived of as a divine woman . . . holy? Never. There is only one truly holy being in the universe, these verses tell us: Yahweh, I AM, the one who is completely other than everything else that exists.

In today's passage Isaiah expresses these ideas in poetic ways. He starts by speaking of the beginning of things. As I said yesterday, the human understanding of reality is remarkably consistent, whether ancient primitive or modern secular humanist. This is the idea that chaotic matter has always existed and will always exist. That makes a lot of sense if this psycho-socio-physical cosmos is all there is. Matter was here before we were born and will be here after we die. Furthermore, if order is let go, it will never become more orderly, it will always tend to become chaotic. But Isaiah says this is not so. There was a moment when this cosmos began; there was a moment when the earth received its foundations. The Hebrews (and we) have been told this, and it is recorded in the book of Genesis. Have we not heard; have we not believed? Please don't get hung up on the question of how many days or hours or years it took. That is not the point. The point is that the human view of reality is wrong. It is not chaotic matter that has always existed; it is that an intelligent, divine Person has always existed, and that this Person *spoke* the cosmos into existence at a certain moment. This is why the big bang theory is so exciting (and why it is so annoying to the secularists). Science confirms what the Bible says: there was a moment when this cosmos began to exist, a moment before which it did not exist!

Isaiah then goes on to picture God enthroned "above the circle of the earth" (v. 22). How interesting! Again, he is speaking poetically of Yahweh's transcendence. He is not of the earth; he is over it. And from that perspective, he has a realistic view of us humans. Earlier he spoke of us as the fragile grass. Now he sees us as less than grasshoppers. Make no mistake: he sees us as the most valuable creatures in the cosmos. But if we get an inflated view of our own powers or significance, we need to be reminded of the heavenly perspective. Then the poet returns to the grass imagery (v. 24). Who will survive on this earth? The princes and mighty men of the world? Those who presume that they can thwart the will of the Transcendent One, the one who calls the stars by name, whom the pagans thought were gods? Of course not! They are nothing more than grass that springs up suddenly and is blown away in an instant. The God who wants to deliver and intends to deliver *can* deliver, and nothing created can stop him.

1. Identify some people, or circumstances, that you honestly think are too much for God to deliver you from. What is it about each that is too much for this God Isaiah is describing?

2. What are some of the evidences you can think of that support the theory of an intelligent designer?

3. What does the theory of chance development (the so-called evolution theory) say to us about the meaning of life?

4. What does the doctrine of transcendence teach us about the possibility of transcending our heredity and environment?

FIVE

He Has Not Forgotten You

Isaiah 40:27–31 *Why do you say, O Jacob, and speak, O Israel, "My way is hidden from the Lord, and my right is disregarded by my God"?* *28Have you not known? Have you not heard? The Lord is the everlasting God, the Creator of the ends of the earth. He does not faint or grow weary; his understanding is unsearchable.* *29He gives power to the faint, and strengthens the powerless.* *30Even youths will faint and be weary, and the young will fall exhausted;* *31but those who wait for the Lord shall renew their strength, they shall mount up with wings like eagles, they shall run and not be weary, they shall walk and not faint.*

Understanding the Word. This final section of Isaiah 40 is a fitting conclusion to the chapter as a whole. It speaks first of all in verse 27 about the discouragement of the exiles. They had thought they were the chosen people of God who would one day rule the world. They had thought that God had promised to bless and preserve them. Now it seemed to them as if God had forgotten all about them and had broken all his promises to them. None of that is true, of course. Their memories, like ours, were very selective. God had not promised that they would rule the world, but that they would be "a kingdom of priests" (Exod. 19:5–6 RSV). That is, they would be the mediators between a lost world and a saving God. Second, they would be God's special possession and would receive his care and protection *if* they kept their side of the covenant. Somehow they had conveniently forgotten that "if." They thought God owed them that care and protection even if they broke every one of the covenant stipulations governing their behavior.

How often we are guilty of the same kind of faulty thinking. We have made a profession of faith; we have joined the church; we have been relatively (sometimes rigorously) faithful in church attendance, and we think that gives us some sort of "lock" on God. Never mind that we are jealous and envious, that we cherish bitterness toward others, that we are stingy toward the poor and outcast, that we are hypercritical, that we are oppressive toward those who work under us. God owes us something, we think. Yes, he does, but it may not be what we think.

But Yahweh does not chide the exiles for these faulty understandings. Rather, he calls attention to who he is. In verses 28 and 29 he says five things about himself that bear on their condition. First, he is the eternal God. That is, he is not conditioned by time. For him, says the apostle Peter, a thousand years is as a day, and a day as a thousand years (2 Peter 3:8). He can do something in a moment that should have taken forever and, as Peter goes on to say (v. 9), he will keep his promise at precisely the right moment.

Second, he is the Creator. This means that he can do something unlike anything that has ever happened before. The so-called gods can never do a new thing; they are doomed to do what they have always done. Imagine the sun coming up in the west some day! Ridiculous! But the infinitely creative one is never hampered by what he has done in the past (Isa. 43:18–19).

Third, standing outside of time and with limitless power, he never gets tired. The gods, being simply humans on a grand scale, may indeed get tired and need some rejuvenation by their human clients. Such a thing is unthinkable for the true God. If he has not yet taken action, it is not because he is tired.

Fourth, he understands everything and so much more. His understanding simply transcends anything we can even conceive of. Sometimes our praying gets a bit ludicrous. We think we have to remind God what the situation is in

11

case he has forgotten, and then we have to tell him how to solve the problem in case he cannot figure that out. The Judeans seem to have been a bit like that: God needs a little coaching to remember just what our condition is here.

Fifth, Yahweh takes particular pleasure in helping the helpless. As Paul says, his strength is shown in our weakness (2 Cor. 12:9). Those who are superior in intelligence, good looks, strength, and wealth all too often foolishly think they do not need God, and in so doing they deprive themselves of all the incredible resources of heaven. Then, when their gifts begin to fail them, they have nowhere to turn. But those who know their need find to their delight that God supplies what is lacking in them.

Thus, we come to the well-known final verse. Since God is all the things I have just enumerated, what is the very best thing we can do? We can wait in eager expectation for the wonderful, unexpected, and creative things God will do on our behalf at the right moment. In the Old Testament *wait* is a frequent synonym of *trust*. This is not waiting simply in the sense of passing time, but rather in the sense of refusing to run ahead of God as though we alone truly know our need and how to meet it. To wait in this sense is to confess both our ignorance and our helplessness, and to throw ourselves on his resources. This is not to counsel passivity as though we do nothing, simply waiting on God to do everything. God will commonly use what abilities and intelligence we have, but it is in his way, not ours; in his time, not ours. I think the order of the verbs here is intentional. Life with God involves moments when we soar, and hours when we run, but most of all it involves a steady, unflagging, purposeful walk with our hands in his.

1. What do we have to give up when we wait for God to take action in our lives?

2. According to this passage, how can we know that God will take action in our lives?

3. Why is "walking" the Christian life more difficult that "soaring"?

COMMENTARY NOTES

The book of Isaiah is centered on the theme of servanthood. Just as Isaiah had his lips cleansed so he could speak a message to the nation, so the nation was to experience a similar fiery cleansing so it could convey God's message to the world. Isaiah had a vision of God's breathtaking holiness—his transcendence (6:1–3), and in many ways that is what chapters 7–39 are about. In those chapters the Holy One of Israel (a favorite title of Isaiah's that only occurs five other times in the Bible, but twenty-six in Isaiah) is displayed as the unique and only ruler of the universe. But the section is also about the need for his servants to trust him completely. They are to trust Yahweh and so be empowered to display his glory to the nations (see 7:4; 12:2; 26:3–4; 30:15, 18; 36:7). Unfortunately, they were more inclined to be seduced by the glory of the nations and so trusted them instead of God. Because of that Isaiah declared that one day they would be taken captive by those very nations that they trusted. In chapters 40–55, we see that this prediction has been fulfilled. The Judean leadership is experiencing the fire of captivity. But just as with the fire that touched Isaiah's lips, God does not intend this experience to destroy them, but rather to cleanse them. In fact, he intends to use the evidence of their experience as proof that he alone is God. Far from casting them off for their sins, he calls them his chosen servants. The final section of the book (chaps. 56–66), probably written to the Judeans

who had returned from captivity, shows what God is going to have to do for them and to them so that they can indeed be a clean lamp through which his light can shine out to the nations (see 60:1–3).

Chapters 40–55 are divided into two sections (41–48, 49–55), with chapter 40 serving as the introduction to the entire unit. Chapters 41–48 deal with deliverance from Babylon, and especially with Yahweh's power to deliver his people from the Babylonian gods. In chapters 41–46 Yahweh again and again calls the gods into court, demanding that they produce evidence to show that they deserve to be called gods. He challenges them to bring witnesses forward who can produce such evidence, and asserts that they cannot do so. Then he calls upon his own people as witnesses on his behalf. The evidence they produce is that Yahweh has indeed specifically predicted future events and those events have occurred. This is something the gods cannot do since they are simply humanized cosmic forces, which cannot know the future.

The second part is chapters 49–55. These chapters deal with a further question about deliverance. Supposing that Yahweh can deliver his people *from* Babylon; how can he deliver them *back* to him? That is, what about the sin that took them to Babylon in the first place and alienated them from him? Is he merely going to act as if those sins had not taken place, as though there had never been a breach in relations between him and them? The answer found in these chapters is that God is going to take their alienation upon himself, and in so doing remove it from the record. Chapters 49:1–52:12 are filled with anticipation of this great deliverance, whereas chapters 54–55 contain a ringing invitation to enter into it. It is 52:13–53:12, the sacrificial death of God's Servant, which accounts for the change from anticipation to invitation.

The years 900–333 BC saw the rise and fall of three great empires in the ancient Near East. The first and third, the Assyrian and the Persian, were relatively long-lived, whereas the second, the Babylonian, was quite short-lived. The Assyrians ruled from 900 to 609 BC. They practiced the policy of exile. That is, when they conquered a people, they resettled the leadership elsewhere in their empire, and brought people in from yet somewhere else to settle in the conquered land. This had at least three effects. The first was terror. You could know that if you resisted the Assyrians and were defeated, you would be dragged off into captivity. The second was to short-circuit rebellions. Why fight for the freedom of a land where you were a stranger? The third was to make it easier to rule an empire full of diverse peoples, cultures, and religions. Exile tended to mix them all up together, to "homogenize" the mass, as it were. The Babylonians, who ruled from 609 to 539, and to whom the nation of Judah had fallen, followed the same practice.

Thus, from 900 until 539, exile had been the rule of the day. During that entire time, no one had ever gone home from exile. To go into exile was to disappear as a distinct people. It fell to the Persians (539–533 BC) under their first emperor, Cyrus, to reverse that practice, just as Isaiah had predicted he would.

Chapter 40 is clearly addressing three questions that Isaiah knew the exiles would be asking. Has God rejected us? Verses 1–11 answer that with a resounding, "No." He loves them and wants to deliver them. But *can* God deliver us? Aren't the Babylonian gods too strong for him? Verses 12–24 again answer, "No." Yahweh is in a class by himself. Those man-made "gods" are not even worthy of the name. In some ways the third question is the most poignant. All right, so God *wants* to deliver us, both from Babylon and from our sins, and he *can* deliver us. Is he actually *going* to deliver us? Here the answer is a resounding, "Of course!"

The terms "Israel" and "Judah" can become a little confusing. Israel is used two ways in the Bible. First, it can be used to refer to the nation as a whole. But second, it can be used to refer to the Northern Kingdom, which came into existence when the kingdom of Solomon broke in two. What was left when that Northern Kingdom broke away was called Judah. Israel, the Northern Kingdom, was destroyed by Assyria in 722 BC, and Judah by Babylon in 586 BC. Isaiah is writing to Judah, which is the remnant of the nation of Israel.

WEEK ONE

GATHERING DISCUSSION OUTLINE

A. Open session in prayer.

B. View video for this week's readings.

C. What general impressions and thoughts do you have after considering the video and reading the daily writings on these scriptures?

D. Discuss questions selected from the daily readings.

    1. **KEY OBSERVATION:** God's response to the people's condition is grace and love.

    DISCUSSION QUESTION: How does this address the common misconception of many people that the God of the Old Testament is a God of wrath?

    2. **KEY OBSERVATION:** God's word is eternal, while humans are as temporary as grass.

    DISCUSSION QUESTION: Why do you think it says that his word is eternal rather than that *he* is eternal?

    3. **KEY OBSERVATION:** Since God is transcendent, he cannot be manipulated by our behavior.

    DISCUSSION QUESTION: What are some of the ways we try to manipulate God?

4. **KEY OBSERVATION:** God cannot be represented in any created form.

   DISCUSSION QUESTION: Why are there no descriptions of Jesus' physical appearance in the New Testament? Suppose there were, what would the result be?

5. **KEY OBSERVATION:** God calls on us to wait for him to take action in our lives.

   DISCUSSION QUESTION: Why does God do this? What are we saying when we won't wait?

E. What facts and information presented in the commentary portion of the lesson help you understand the weekly scripture?

F. Close session with prayer.

WEEK TWO

Isaiah 41:1–14, 21–29

The Fearful Servant

INTRODUCTION

Does our world seem in chaos to you today? Someone has called the twentieth century the most chaotic in the history of the world, and it certainly seemed to have a good claim to be that. Now we are in a new century, and although we are not fighting a world war, it certainly seems that the legacy of violence is rearing its ugly head in every part of the globe today. It must have been like that for the people of Judah in the century between 625 and 525 BC. The events of that one hundred years convulsed the whole world they knew, and must have seemed cataclysmic to them. Assyria, which had dominated that world for more than 250 years, reached its height about 650 BC. It was all that the people of the ancient Near East had ever known and must have seemed eternal. Yet, hardly twenty-five years after that peak moment, Assyria's supposedly impregnable capital fell in a matter of months, and in another fifteen years, the Assyrian Empire did not exist. What an upheaval!

Assyria had been brought down by a coalition of two old enemies: Babylon, the wealthy, sophisticated city to the south, and the Medes, warring tribes in the mountains to the east, who had successfully resisted all of Assyria's attempts to conquer them. So it seemed from 609 BC onward that Babylon would establish a new, multi-century empire. But it was not to be. The Babylonian Empire was really the creation of one man: Nebuchadnezzar, and with his death in 562, it all began to unravel. The Medes left the Babylonian fold and joined with the Persians to the south, and together they began to eat away at Babylon's holdings so that after only a seventy-year duration, the Babylonian Empire fell, to be replaced by yet a third empire: the Persian. All this, from Assyria to Persia, took place in about an eighty-five-year span. It is no wonder that this chapter of Isaiah is marked by repetition of the word "fear."

So how shall we handle our fears in a world exponentially more complicated than the one that the Judeans faced? Although our world is more complicated, the answers are the same for us as they were for the Judeans. If we will learn what the Judeans were to have learned, our world will still be complicated and uncertain, but we will be able to live confidently and securely in the midst of all its unknowns.

ONE

Fears That Assail Us

Isaiah 41:1–7 *Listen to me in silence, O coastlands; let the peoples renew their strength; let them approach, then let them speak; let us together draw near for judgment.*

²Who has roused a victor from the east, summoned him to his service? He delivers up nations to him, and tramples kings under foot; he makes them like dust with his sword, like driven stubble with his bow. ³He pursues them and passes on safely, scarcely touching the path with his feet. ⁴Who has performed and done this, calling the generations from the beginning? I, the LORD, am first, and will be with the last. ⁵The coastlands have seen and are afraid, the ends of the earth tremble; they have drawn near and come. ⁶Each one helps the other, saying to one another, "Take courage!" ⁷The artisan encourages the goldsmith, and the one who smooths with the hammer encourages the one who strikes the anvil, saying of the soldering, "It is good"; and they fasten it with nails so that it cannot be moved.

Understanding the Word. Verse 1 is a summons into the courtroom. As such it sets the stage for much of what follows through chapter 46. There is no clear outline for the material, but rather a continued repetition of certain themes, all related to the assertion that Yahweh is the only being worthy of the title "God." Central to all this, as stated in Week One, is the challenge to the gods to present evidence that would support their claims to divinity. We will see that challenge first stated explicitly later in this chapter. This summons into court is issued to the whole world, since "coastlands" refers to the ends of the earth. Some may have thought that Yahweh was simply the god of Israel, but that is not what he says; he is the God of the world.

The centerpiece of Yahweh's argument for his own uniqueness is that he raised up Cyrus (vv. 2, 25), and that he predicted it far in advance, even to the extent of naming the conqueror when no one knew who he was. No idol-god could have done such a thing, for it was something and someone brand-new, something and someone unheard of before. Here is the first step to the mastery of our fears. Our God has all things, including the future, well in hand. Nothing that is going to happen will be a surprise to him; nor will it confound him. This is not to say that we believe in a deterministic God, like Allah, who directly causes everything that happens. Rather, we believe that there are processes that take place as a result of the cause-and-effect principles that God has built into his creation. God normally permits these to follow their regular courses; *however*, he is able to alter them, intervene in them, or even suspend them if it suits his larger purposes. And in any case, as Romans 8:28 teaches us, he can use any of them for the greater good. He is the first and will be there at the end (Isa. 41:4). So we need not fear; history is in God's hand, and he is guiding it to its appointed goals.

But when the worldling looks at the Persian conqueror trampling "kings under foot" (v. 2), he or she does not have this confidence. This person must try to construct something for himself or herself to defeat the fears. Here the terror-stricken people set about constructing new idols (vv. 5–7). The picture of them encouraging one another is so pathetic because it is so futile. We may not make god statues to calm our fears, but all too often we, too, turn for support to other kinds of devices that are no less of our own making. As in 40:19–20, and much more fully in 44:9–20, Isaiah is here graphically sarcastic in speaking of the folly of idol making. The makers have to choose a special wood so the idol will not rot and fall over (40:20), or they have to nail it down (41:7). And this is supposed to take care of them!

1. What are some of the fears that you are facing?

2. What are some of the things that we "manufacture" to help us conquer our fears?

3. What are some of the evidences (ancient and modern) that God is in control of history?

TWO

He Is with Us

Isaiah 41:8–10 *But you, Israel, my servant, Jacob, whom I have chosen, the offspring of Abraham, my friend; ⁹you whom I took from the ends of the earth, and called from its farthest corners, saying to you, "You are my servant, I have chosen you and not cast you off"; ¹⁰do not fear, for I am with you, do not be afraid, for I am your God; I will strengthen you, I will help you, I will uphold you with my victorious right hand.*

Understanding the Word. Although these are three separate verses in Hebrew, they constitute a single thought as they are usually translated into English. They begin with a lengthy identification of the person being addressed that extends through the first half of verse 9. Then the address is found in the rest of verse 9 and verse 10. The point is that while the rest of the world is horrified by what they see this new conqueror doing, and what they fear it is going to mean for the established structures of their world, Israel can rest securely. That is actually a bit shocking, because if any people had reason to fear, it was the exiled Israelites. They had a double reason to be afraid. First, they were afraid they would be absorbed into the culture of the empire and would cease to exist as a people. Second, as the lowest of the low in society, they were more vulnerable than anyone else in the evident upcoming devastations. Yet Yahweh told them not to be afraid. Why do they, helpless as they are, not need to fear?

The answer lies in two things: who they are, and who Yahweh is. In the light of those two things, they can live confidently even while the world is seemingly about to fall about their ears. Who are they? They are the recipients of the unbelievable grace of God, his passionate devotion to them, which they do not deserve at all. They believe the exile is evidence that God has cast them off (v. 9), that all the promises have been nullified. But he says it is not so. They are his chosen servants. The ancient promises to Abraham and to Jacob were just as much true then as when he first made them. The pagans may only have "now," but God's people are part of a long history of gracious salvation. In Abraham, Yahweh had gathered them from Chaldea, the very place where they now found themselves, so he could certainly gather them back again. And

Jacob? The old scoundrel? If God had chosen to redeem and use that man, then he certainly could redeem and use them.

Who are you? You, too, are the chosen servant of God; chosen before the world began, according to Ephesians 1:4. You, too, whoever you are, are not cast off, however you may have failed him in the past. Do not take counsel of such fears. Just as he said to the exiled Judean, he says to us, "I am with you." What does that mean as regards our fears? It means we are never alone, not in the darkest night nor in the fiercest battle. But what does that mean? The hymn writer said it well, "Fear not, I am with thee; O, be not dismayed. For I am thy God and will still give thee aid. I'll comfort thee, help thee, and cause thee to stand, upheld by my righteous, omnipotent hand" ("How Firm a Foundation," 1787). God's presence means that we have resources to face persecution (I can stand with my Lord), or loss (he, and his approval, are what I really need), or even death (he will take me home). Without that sense of his presence, we are left to our own resources, and those are never enough in crisis hours. With him we will still suffer, we will still have unanswered questions; but the deep consciousness of him at our side, and even better, in our hearts, will mean that we know all will be right in the end. With that assurance we can face whatever comes with our heads up.

1. Think of a time as a child when you were very frightened, and one or both of your parents came to you. Describe your feelings.

2. What are some of the things you know are true if God is with you?

3. Think of something you are afraid of. Now imagine God holding your hand as you face that fear. What does he say about it?

THREE

I Will Help You

Isaiah 41:11–14 *Yes, all who are incensed against you shall be ashamed and disgraced; those who strive against you shall be as nothing and shall perish. [12]You shall seek those who contend with you, but you shall not find them; those who war against you shall be as nothing at all. [13]For I, the Lord your God, hold your right hand; it is I who say to you, "Do not fear, I will help you."*

¹⁴Do not fear, you worm Jacob, you insect Israel! I will help you, says the LORD; *your Redeemer is the Holy One of Israel.*

Understanding the Word. The promise that God was making to his people here, as recorded in verses 11 and 12, must have seemed well-nigh unbelievable. Mighty Babylon, Daniel's empire of gold (Dan. 2:37–38), would disappear? Surely not! Yet, again and again across the centuries, God has done this very thing for his people. One of the greatest persecutions of the church took place under the Roman emperor Diocletian in the closing years of the third century AD. It must have seemed to Christians at that time, when thousands of them were being killed, that the church could not survive. Yet in fewer than twenty-five years, the emperor Constantine was converted and the official religion of the Roman Empire became Christianity.

So it was with Babylon. Fewer than twenty-five years after Nebuchadnezzar's death, his empire ceased to exist. The mighty king who had destroyed Jerusalem when it dared to rebel against him was gone, and all the power and wealth of which he boasted (Dan. 4:28–30) was gone as well. Babylon had been God's tool to discipline his people, but despite Nebuchadnezzar's vacillating professions of faith, as recorded in Daniel, it is clear that the Babylonians never saw themselves that way. They could not believe that the god of little Judah could possibly be the Judge of the whole earth, as Abraham had in Genesis 18:25.

Sometimes the challenges we face seem to be absolutely insurmountable. But when we think that way, we have forgotten God. This is often the strategy of our enemy. He tries to get us to think like "practical atheists," those who say they believe in God, but think and act as though he does not exist. Remember that whatever you are facing, God is bigger. He will probably solve your problem in a very different way than you imagine, but your task is to not give up hope, but rather, to keep living in the knowledge that God exists, that he cares for you, and that nothing is insoluble for him.

In this passage we find the second reason that we do not need to fear when we face difficulty and uncertainty. The first reason, as we saw yesterday, is that God is with us—we do not face these things alone. The second reason is that Yahweh, the Creator of the universe, will help us. This is an amazing statement. He does not tell us just to sit down and watch an expert do the work. He says that he is going to get in the situation with us. Why would he do that? He could do it so much more easily by himself. And sometimes we would like that. It would free us from the responsibility. But no, he thinks too much of us to do it that way. The parent who works with his or her child does that not because it is the most efficient way to accomplish the task, but because the parent values the child and also the experience of being with the child. God is the same way: he values us too much simply to do the work for us. He wants us to be involved with him in solving the problem. He wants to be involved with us in whatever it is that needs doing, and sometimes the involvement is the most important thing that takes place. On the other hand, he does not ask us to perform the task while he watches. He knows that our strength is too small for the task; he knows that our vision is too narrow to see what needs to be done. So he comes alongside; he says, "You start, and I'll supply the strength," or, "You try, and I will show you where we need to go."

1. Think of some examples, besides those we've already discussed, where God has done the seemingly impossible.

2. What are some examples, perhaps in your own life, of "practical atheism"?

3. How has God helped you accomplish some things that you could not have done on your own?

FOUR

Making the Right Choices

Isaiah 41:21–24 *Set forth your case, says the LORD; bring your proofs, says the King of Jacob. ²²Let them bring them, and tell us what is to happen. Tell us the former things, what they are, so that we may consider them, and that we may know their outcome; or declare to us the things to come. ²³Tell us what is to come hereafter, that we may know that you are gods; do good, or do harm, that we may be afraid and terrified. ²⁴You, indeed, are nothing and your work is nothing at all; whoever chooses you is an abomination.*

Understanding the Word. Here is the first place where Yahweh calls on the Babylonian gods to present evidence that they are gods. (See the commentary for further discussion of this feature.) Notice that he identifies himself as "the King of Jacob" (v. 21). Throughout the entire book of Isaiah, God delights to define himself in relation to his people. The Babylonians may think of these people from Judah as nothing and nobody, people who could not protect themselves, and worse, people whose god could not protect them. But God loves to identify himself by reference to them. So he is "the Holy One *of Israel*," or "the Mighty One *of Jacob*." The mightiest being in the universe has taken these people to his heart and chooses to identify himself by that relationship. That is what he has done with the church and with you and me. The world may look upon the church of Jesus Christ with contempt. So often we are rent with dissension, or troubled with pettiness or legalism, foolishly proud of our righteousness, but God calls us his own, his special possession. It is the same with each of us who names the name of Christ. How often we fail him; how often we fall short of even our own little goals, yet he delights to call himself "the God of _____," and we can each fill in the blank. He has chosen us.

But whom have we chosen? The Babylonians, and all the other peoples of the ancient world, with the exception of the Israelites (but all too often, they too), had chosen to worship this world and its forces. They chose to worship power, and called it Baal, or Hadad, or Marduk, or Hercules. They chose to worship passion, and called it Inanna, or Ishtar, or Asherah, or Aphrodite. They chose to worship wisdom and called it Thoth, or Ea, or Kothar-wa-Khasis. Sadly, people of the twenty-first century are not any different. One has only to look at our media to know that we, too, worship the forces of this earth, whether it be power, or passion, or the intellect. We have taken the masks off the gods, but they are the same gods. And tragically, they are just as useless in the end. They cannot explain where they came from, and when we are old, they desert us, leaving us helpless and alone. They pretend to give our lives meaning, but in the end, death makes a mockery of them all. Only the one who stands outside of the rolling wheel of time can tell us where we came from and what we are made for. Only the Creator deserves all our allegiance. This is the significance of verse 24: "whoever chooses you is an abomination." An abomination is something that is contrary to creation order; to try to use any created thing to do what only the Creator can do is abominable. We were not made to do that.

1. What does it mean to you that Yahweh, "I AM," chooses to be your God?

2. What are some of the created things that people try to use to give meaning to their lives?

3. What are some examples of abominable choices?

F I V E

Telling the Future

Isaiah 41:25–29 *I stirred up one from the north, and he has come, from the rising of the sun he was summoned by name. He shall trample on rulers as on mortar, as the potter treads clay. [26]Who declared it from the beginning, so that we might know, and beforehand, so that we might say, "He is right"? There was no one who declared it, none who proclaimed, none who heard your words. [27]I first have declared it to Zion, and I give to Jerusalem a herald of good tidings. [28]But when I look there is no one; among these there is no counselor who, when I ask, gives an answer. [29]No, they are all a delusion; their works are nothing; their images are empty wind.*

Understanding the Word. This passage is about two things: Yahweh's lordship over history and his ability to tell the future. With the passage from yesterday, it is the first of the cases against the gods. Yahweh insists that he alone can tell in advance what he is going to do in history. In this case he had foretold that he was going to raise up the Persian emperor Cyrus, who would trample down the Babylonian Empire. Had any of the gods ever done anything like this? Never. Oh, the omen priests might tell the king that if he would go to battle on a day when six black birds had flown east, he would be victorious (unless while he was marching, five white birds happened to fly west), but that is a far cry from the kind of specific prediction that Yahweh could and did make. He stands outside of time and can see all the events of time at once.

But we need to be careful when we think about prophecy. I was teaching an adult Sunday school class several years ago, and we had come to the end of one topic, so I asked the class what they would like to study next. The consensus was that they would like to study prophecy. So I led them into a study of the book of Amos. After three or four weeks, I began to get some strange looks from the class members. Finally, I stopped and asked them what was the matter. They said, "We thought we were going to study prophecy." What was the problem? When they thought of prophecy, they thought of the last chapters of Daniel and Zechariah, Ezekiel 38 and 39, and the book of Revelation. They thought prophecy was God telling us what was going to happen in the future. Well, that certainly is a part of prophecy, but it is a rather small part, and the way it works is not quite the way we think. Most of the prophetic books are calls to the people of the prophet's own time. They are usually either calls to repent of their sins, or calls to believe God's promises. Then the prophet usually gives them a choice of what their future will be. If they repent or believe, then the future will be this. But if they won't repent or believe, then the future will be that. In other words, for the Old Testament prophets, *we* determine what our future will be. This is not to say that our bad choices and their sad results will thwart God's ultimate plan to save the world. If we will not respond to his call, he will have to go around another way, and he may have to use someone else instead of us, but he *will* accomplish his good purposes.

So what is happening here? God had announced that Israel and Judah would go into exile unless they repented. But he said that he would still keep his ancient promise to Abraham. So he promised to deliver them from exile and said he would do it through a pagan emperor who did not even know Yahweh's name. Had a pagan god ever done anything like all of that? Of course not!

1. What is the purpose of predicting the future in the Prophets?

2. How should we not use the prophetic writings?

3. How *should* we use the prophetic writings?

COMMENTARY NOTES

Chapter 41 opens the section on deliverance from Babylon (chaps. 41–48). The section has two parts: chapters 41–46, and chapters 47–48. The first section deals with Yahweh's case against the gods, and his use of Israel as his witnesses in that case. Again and again, Yahweh asserts that he is God and there is no other. The proof of that is his ability to specifically predict the future. By the close of chapter 46, it is abundantly clear that the Babylonian gods are not divine at all in any meaningful sense of the term. Thus, there is no barrier to God's deliverance of his people from the grip of Babylon. That leads to the second part: the conclusion. Chapter 47 is addressed to Babylon. She must come down from her proud throne and sit in the dust. She is under judgment by the one God of the universe. Chapter 48 is addressed to Israel. They must continue to listen to God's promises of deliverance. As is the case everywhere in the Bible, "to listen" is to take appropriate action on what is said. Here the appropriate action is to maintain active faith in Yahweh so that they do not settle down in Babylon, but are ready to depart at a moment's notice.

The "victor from the east" (v. 2) and the "one from the north" (v. 25) are the same person. Both refer to Cyrus, the first emperor of the Persian Empire. The homeland of Persia was in the southern area of what is now Iran, east of Babylon, that was centered on the Euphrates River in what is now central Iraq. Cyrus, assisted by the Medes, from the mountainous northwest of Iran, overthrew the Babylonian Empire in 538 BC. Although his home was east of Babylon, his campaigns leading up to the final conquest were all carried out in the northern part of Babylon's territories, so that he did come from the north for the final battle. The naming of "Cyrus" by Isaiah (44:28; 45:1) is one of the important pieces in the argument for Yahweh's uniqueness. (See Day Five.)

The significance of Yahweh's claim that the pagan gods cannot predict specific events in the future, while he can (41:21–29), is not immediately apparent to most of us who have no knowledge of pagan religion. As I said in Week One, Day Four, paganism is marked by the conviction that the present psycho-socio-physical cosmos is all there is to reality. There is nothing beyond it. This means that the cosmos is without purpose or plan, having always existed, coming from nowhere and going nowhere. It also means that all existence is circular, with no past or future, but simply now. Everything that has happened will happen again, and everything that will happen has already happened. It is thus impossible to predict some specific event in the future that in any way differs from what has always happened. The presence of destructive forces in the cosmos is explained as being the result of the struggle between two eternally existing forces in the cosmos, one constructive and the other destructive. This is not to say one is "right" and the other is "wrong." It is simply the nature of existence. That means that finally there are no moral absolutes. Nothing is absolutely right or absolutely wrong. It is simply a matter of deciding what works or doesn't work in a particular situation.

As I said in the previous lesson, this philosophy of reality pervaded the ancient world. But in fact, it pervades the world, east and west, ancient and modern. There is only one place where an opposing view is put forward; it is in the Old Testament, and is expressed in the three cultures derived from that book: Judaism, Christianity, and Islam. (Muhammad was clearly influenced by both Judaism and Christianity before he started his own religion. There is no other likely source for many of his ideas, including monotheism and iconoclasm, than the Bible.)

What is that view? Yahweh alone, who is entirely distinct from the cosmos, created the cosmos on purpose and for a purpose—namely, that he might have a love relationship with human beings, his highest creatures, who were endowed with personhood like his. Because of that purpose, these beings were made with the possibility of defying him and rejecting such a relationship. Evil is thus not inherent in the cosmos, but is a consequence of our choosing that option. And since our first parents chose that option, destructive forces have been unleashed in the cosmos. There are thus moral absolutes: those things which reflect God's character lead to fulfilling life; those

which do not reflect his character lead to dissolution and death.

But what about predicting the future? The gods cannot predict specific, unique events because they are only humanized cosmic forces. They cannot tell where they came from or what life is about ("the former things," Isa. 41:22), nor can they tell us what will happen in the future (v. 23) that is anything other than a repetition of what has already occurred. But Yahweh can! He "sits above the circle of the earth" (40:22) and is thus able to see all the course of history from beginning to end. Furthermore, as the transcendent Creator, he can do new things that have never happened before. The argument is, then, that only a being who is genuinely other than the cosmos has a right to be called divine, and that these beings who are manifestly part of the cosmos, since they do not know the future, have no such right.

There were two reasons why the Israelites did not believe the prophets when they predicted the exile and then when they predicted that God's people would be delivered from exile. Both are related to the topic just discussed. The Israelites' thinking was heavily infected with the pagan understanding of reality. They understood that God had made a covenant with them that included the promise of the land of Canaan forever. So that is the way things are and will always be, they thought. They could not imagine any way that they could be driven out of the land and still be God's chosen people. The two could not go together in the world as they conceived it. Furthermore, from the pagan point of view, God needed them. He needed them to feed him with their sacrifices; he needed them to maintain the temple so that he would have a place to live. So, no, the prophets were wrong when they predicted the exile. It was an impossibility in the world as they understood it.

And *if* by some chance they *did* go into exile, it was *more* than impossible that they would ever return. That was so for two reasons. The first was the very purpose of exile: to destroy the distinctive character of a people and to acculturate them to the bland cultural mishmash that characterized the empire. So it was foolish to imagine that the culture of the people of Israel and Judah would somehow survive that. It would be a new thing, and new things don't happen in a cosmos where there is nothing and no one outside that cosmos. The second reason rested on the same assumption: in the 450 years that exile had been practiced, no people had ever gone home. So if it hadn't happened yet, it was *never* going to happen! No wonder the exiles were so afraid (41:10, 13–14).

But that was exactly God's point: through his prophets he had predicted two things that were impossible on the pagan view of things, two things that had come to pass or were about to. What did that mean? It meant that the pagan view of things was wrong! It meant that he was an entirely different order of being from those things that the world called "gods."

WEEK TWO

GATHERING DISCUSSION OUTLINE

A. Open session in prayer.

B. View video for this week's readings.

C. What general impressions and thoughts do you have after considering the video and reading the daily writings on these scriptures?

D. Discuss questions selected from the daily readings.

1. **KEY OBSERVATION:** Our fears often keep us from trusting God.

   DISCUSSION QUESTION: What are some of the "non-God" things we are tempted to rely on to control our fears?

2. **KEY OBSERVATION:** God is with us.

   DISCUSSION QUESTION: What are some of the things that we know are so if God is with us?

3. **KEY OBSERVATION:** God promises to hold our hands and help us.

   DISCUSSION QUESTION: What are some examples, perhaps in your own life, of "practical atheism"?

4. **KEY OBSERVATION:** To treat the forces of this world as though they were God is to commit an abomination.

   DISCUSSION QUESTION: What are some of the created things that people try to use to create meaning in their lives?

5. **KEY OBSERVATION:** God does not predict the future in the prophets so that we can create a "timetable."

   DISCUSSION QUESTION: What is the purpose of God's predicting the future in the Prophets?

E. What facts and information presented in the commentary portion of the lesson help you understand the weekly scripture?

F. Close session with prayer.

WEEK THREE

Isaiah 42:1–22; 43:1–7

Servants: Delivering and Captive

INTRODUCTION

In last week's passage we were introduced to the fearful servant, one who had been taken from home, was forced to live in an alien environment, and was faced with the very real possibility that his or her culture and people would simply be absorbed into the great empire in which they lived. This week we will learn more about that servant, whom we can now call the "captive servant." But between the fearful servant of chapter 41 and the captive servant of 42:18–43:7, we are introduced to another servant, one who is neither fearful nor captive, but rather has a mission of deliverance. While some believe that this description is actually the same person as the fearful and the captive, but just at a different point in time (see the commentary that follows), I am going to argue that it is not the same person. The one servant needs deliverance, from Babylon, yes, and Cyrus will be the means of that deliverance. But much more critically, that servant needs deliverance from the alienation from God that sin had produced, and simply getting back to the land of Israel would not solve that problem. It is by means of this second servant that that problem will be solved, a matter that will mostly be discussed in chapters 49–55. But perhaps you are saying, "Well, if that's true, why are we hearing about that other servant here, where the main issue is captivity in Babylon?" Good question! The answer, I think, is that the two problems are interrelated and Isaiah wants to introduce us to the ultimate solution before we get too far along.

ONE

The Delivering Servant's Character

Isaiah 42:1–4 *Here is my servant, whom I uphold, my chosen, in whom my soul delights; I have put my spirit upon him; he will bring forth justice to the nations. ²He will not cry or lift up his voice, or make it heard in the street; ³a bruised reed he will not break, and a dimly burning wick he will not quench; he will faithfully bring forth justice. ⁴He will not grow faint or be crushed until he has established justice in the earth; and the coastlands wait for his teaching.*

Understanding the Word. In these verses we have a very densely packed description of this delivering servant's character, and I would like to suggest that it gives us a remarkably good model of the kind of person God is looking for in the world. Notice first of all that this servant is not self-standing; he is upheld by God. What does that mean? Among other things it means that such a person is not alone, a condition God never intended for anyone. He made us for relationship, first of all, with himself. It also means that such a person is not limited to his or her own resources—all the resources of heaven are right at hand.

Second, we see that this person, like the fearful and captive servant, is also chosen. What that means is that our relationship with God is never accidental, or worse, unintended. God knows every one of us intimately, and draws us into relationship with him completely intentionally. Whoever you may be, know that God personally selects you for his own.

Third, this person brings delight to God in the deepest parts of his personality. "Soul" in verse 1 is a translation of a Hebrew word that really has no equivalent in English. It might be translated "personality," but it is deeper than that. So it might be translated "self," but that is a bit impersonal. It is the person's inmost self, that which makes you, you. That is the place in God that is touched by this person. I want to be that sort of person, don't you?

Fourth, God's Spirit is on this person. Yes, he or she is upheld by God, chosen by God, a deeply felt delight to God, but how is all that possible? Surely not as a product of the flawed human spirit. The tragedies of the Old Testament are a testimony to how deeply flawed our spirits, the motivating drive within us, really are. If we are to experience the life of God, as this person does, then we, too, will have to have an infusion of his life-giving Spirit. Fortunately, since Christ has come, the Spirit is not only for the select few, as in Old Testament days, but for all of us who will name the name of Christ (see Romans 8:9–11).

Then this person has a passion to see God's divine order, his justice (see the commentary that follows), flourishing in the world. We may not be able to "bring forth justice to the nations," as this servant was to do (Isa. 42:1), but if we share the characteristics mentioned earlier, then this will be our passion. We will want to see all people treated with equity and integrity, but beyond that we will long for love to reign in the world on every level, beginning with those closest to us.

There are two more characteristics mentioned here that are vitally important. The first is the servant's attitude. It is not self-assertive. His world-changing mission would not be accomplished by putting himself, his opinions, his rights, out there in front of everyone. He does not have to get his way. In the end, that is the bottom line of the human sin problem: "I will have my way!" Not this servant. Someone has said, "There is no limit to what God can do with you if you don't care who gets the glory."

The final characteristic of this servant is seen in verse 4. Lack of self-assertion does not mean weakness or lack of confidence. It is just confidence in God rather than oneself. It is also the confidence that the one whose identity is secure in God may be put down, but never put out.

1. Which of these characteristics do you find it most difficult to emulate? Why?

2. What needs to happen in your life to make these characteristics more practically real?

3. There has been a great deal of emphasis recently on the need to be self-assertive. How does the teaching here relate to that? How is biblical non-self-assertion not the same as becoming a doormat?

TWO

The Mission of the Delivering Servant

Isaiah 42:5–9 *Thus says God, the* LORD, *who created the heavens and stretched them out, who spread out the earth and what comes from it, who gives breath to the people upon it and spirit to those who walk in it:* *⁶I am the* LORD, *I have called you in righteousness, I have taken you by the hand and kept you; I have given you as a covenant to the people, a light to the nations,* *⁷to open the eyes that are blind, to bring out the prisoners from the dungeon, from the prison those who sit in darkness.* *⁸I am the* LORD, *that is my name; my glory I give to no other, nor my praise to idols.* *⁹See, the former things have come to pass, and new things I now declare; before they spring forth, I tell you of them.*

Understanding the Word. These verses give us the second part of the message about the delivering servant. In the first part (vv. 1–4) the prophet was describing the servant. But now Yahweh himself weighs in (vv. 5–9), explaining how his nature and character affect the mission of the servant.

Verses 5–9 are remarkable for the number of divine assertions that are to be found in them. Yahweh begins (v. 5) by stating that he is the Creator both of the physical universe and also the one who gives life to human beings. This is directly related to the mission of the servant that began to be alluded to in the previous passage. In verses 1, 3–4, it was said that this servant will bring "justice," that is, divine order, to the earth. But "justice," or order, can be a very slippery thing. Who determines what justice or order is? You? Me? The Democrats? The Republicans? Babylon? None of the above! It is only the Creator of the universe, the Life Giver, who is in a position to say, "*This* is how I made the world to operate. *This* is what has gone awry. *This* is the way to restore it all." Then, in verses 8 and 9, he insists that he alone *can* restore the world to what it was meant to be. He is I AM, Yahweh, the Source, the basis, and the end of all existence, the only self-existent being in the universe. The idol gods cannot do anything other than that which has always been. If there is evil and disorder in the world, if it seems that all order is sooner or later collapsing into chaos, that is because that is the way things have always been, and nothing will ever change. But the glory of the transcendent God, something he will never share with a humanly designed idol (v. 8), is that he can do something brand-new (v. 9). Just because we humans have never known a world without evil, corruption, oppression, and violence does not mean it can never be changed. The transcendent Creator can change it back to the way he designed it to be in the beginning.

So where does the servant's mission come into all this? It is in verses 6–7. God has particularly chosen this person, and he was absolutely right in doing so (v. 6), to set the prisoners free (v. 7). Prisoners of whom? Babylon? No, much more than that. As the context shows, people are prisoners of a world dominated by the disorder, the injustice, that is a result of sin. This servant is going to set us free from that! How will he do so? He will be a "covenant to the people" (v. 6). The full explanation of that must come later. But here at the outset, we can say that the Sinai covenant had been broken and broken and broken, and as such its legal demand was that the people must be destroyed. If something new was to come into the world, that covenant was going to have to be satisfied. In some way, this servant was going to do that, and in so doing become "a light to the nations" (v. 6).

1. Why is God able to do a new thing when the gods of this world cannot?

2. What new thing do you need God in Christ to do in your life? Do you think he can? Why or why not?

3. When God restores his order in human relationships, what does it look like?

THREE

The Heart of God

Isaiah 42:10–17 *Sing to the LORD a new song, his praise from the end of the earth! Let the sea roar and all that fills it, the coastlands and their inhabitants. ¹¹Let the desert and its towns lift up their voice, the villages that Kedar inhabits; let the inhabitants of Sela sing for joy, let them shout from the tops of the mountains. ¹²Let them give glory to the LORD, and declare his praise in the coastlands. ¹³The LORD goes forth like a soldier, like a warrior he stirs up his fury; he cries out, he shouts aloud, he shows himself mighty against his foes.*

¹⁴For a long time I have held my peace, I have kept still and restrained myself; now I will cry out like a woman in labor, I will gasp and pant. ¹⁵I will lay waste mountains and hills, and dry up all their herbage; I will turn the rivers into islands, and dry up the pools. ¹⁶I will lead the blind by a road they do not know, by paths they have not known I will guide them. I will turn the darkness before them into light, the rough places into level ground. These are the things I will do, and I will not forsake them. ¹⁷They shall be turned back and utterly put to shame— those who trust in carved images, who say to cast images, "You are our gods."

Understanding the Word. This passage is composed of two parts. The first is an ecstatic song of praise for what the delivering servant will have done (vv. 10–12). The second is a lyrical statement of God's intentions for his people. It is as though we get a glimpse here into the saving heart of God that was revealed in his calling of the delivering servant.

Verses 10–12 are a strong argument that the ministry of the delivering servant was to be of a universal character. We are not merely talking about a redeemed Israel's demonstration of God's goodness to them. Verses 10 and 12 state that the entire earth is to be caught up in the celebration. ("Coastlands" refer to the ends of the earth.) Both the chaotic sea and the apparently lifeless desert are called upon to join in. (Kedar and Sela are locations southeast of the Dead Sea, on the fringes of the Arabian Desert.) Then it is the lowlands of the desert and the heights of the mountains that are challenged to take part in this "new song" (v. 10). All of this is in honor of the new thing that God will do as a manifestation of his sole glory in the ministry of the servant.

What is it that accounts for this world-changing ministry, this restoration of the divine order in the world? Ultimately, it comes from the heart of Yahweh. As Ezekiel tells us, God gets "no pleasure from the death of anyone" (Ezek. 18:32), and the New Testament chimes in with "[He does not want] any to perish" (2 Peter 3:9). That truth is expressed in this lyrical outburst that Isaiah hears from the mouth of Yahweh. If only the exile came at long last, when God's incredible patience had finally come to an end, now he says he has been patient long enough with the bondage of his people (v. 14), and cries out that he wants to take on their enemies, (both physical and spiritual bondage here, I think), like a warrior going into battle (see also Isaiah 59:15–21; 63:1–6). Then he changes the figure of speech: he is like a pregnant woman determined to push past all the pain and fatigue and deliver her child (v. 14). This is a glimpse into the heart of God. How deeply does he feel the tragedy of our condition, and how determined is he to find a way out of it for us? *This* deeply and *this* determined.

But this kind of deliverance will require him to do something new, something no idol could even dream of, much less do (see verse 17). The gods of this world can never offer us real deliverance from whatever enchains us. The best that modern secular humanism can put forward is self-realization; just become more of who you really are. There is not much hope there. But Yahweh can do the impossible: he can dry up rivers, flatten mountains, make the blind see, turn darkness into light (vv. 15–16). In the history of the Christian faith, this story has been played out a million times, as God has transformed drunkards to sober citizens, haters to lovers, hopeless to hopeful, fearful to courageous. He can do a new thing.

1. Why do we often feel that God does not care about our needs?

2. What other passages can you think of that teach us about God's desire and determination to be gracious toward us?

3. What are some of the things God has done in your life that were really impossible?

FOUR

Blind and Deaf

Isaiah 42:18–22 *Listen, you that are deaf; and you that are blind, look up and see! ¹⁹Who is blind but my servant, or deaf like my messenger whom I send? Who is blind like my dedicated one, or blind like the servant of the LORD? ²⁰He sees many things, but does not observe them; his ears are open, but he does not hear. ²¹The LORD was pleased, for the sake of his righteousness, to magnify his teaching and make it glorious. ²²But this is a people robbed and plundered, all of them are trapped in holes and hidden in prisons; they have become a prey with no one to rescue, a spoil with no one to say, "Restore!"*

Understanding the Word. Here is the servant of Yahweh again, but as I contended earlier, and in the commentary that follows, this is not the servant that was described in 42:1–9. That servant was alert and sensitive, confident and gifted with power to deliver. This servant is blind and deaf, and as a result has been robbed and trapped. Who is this servant? And maybe even more to the point, how can this person *be* God's servant? As to the servant's identity, it seems very clear that this is the nation of Israel. At the outset of his ministry, as reported in chapter 6, Isaiah had received a strange, even shocking, commission. He was told to preach a message that would deafen and blind his hearers, and would make their hearts hard (6:9–10).

What was that about? Surely God wants people to hear his truth and see what he is doing in the world, and to turn to him with softened hearts, doesn't he? So why would he tell Isaiah to do this?

I think the answer is this: there was a cancer at work in God's people. It would take the Northern Kingdom, Israel, into captivity during Isaiah's lifetime, and was already far advanced in the Southern Kingdom, Judah. It would take another 150 years to reach its deadly fulfillment there in the south, but its progress already looked inevitable.

What was that cancer? It was essentially a paganization of the worship of Yahweh. That is, Yahweh is the top god, and he has chosen us to be his. He has committed himself to us in a covenant, and this means that if we keep him happy with a beautiful temple and lots of sacrifices, we can get him to bless us and take care of us. In short, God exists to meet our needs, and we just have to know how to manipulate him. Of course, there are other gods too, and sometimes they meet our needs better than Yahweh does, so we need to do "side deals" with them from time to time. They had completely misunderstood what the Torah (or, "teaching" in verse 21) was about.

God had given the covenant to them so that in an exclusive relationship of obedience to him, they could learn his righteous character and come to understand that he wants to give that same character to us humans. But the people thought that the covenant was some sort of genie's lamp that they could rub just right to get the genie to grant their wishes. So Isaiah had a choice: he could preach a message that would be acceptable to people with that sort of cancer, one that might earn him a good-sized following; or he could faithfully declare the word of Yahweh, knowing that it would actually turn that generation away from the truth and harden them in their pagan convictions. He chose the latter course, and that is exactly what happened (see Isaiah 8:16–22). But by being faithful, his message of truth and righteousness would be available to a later generation. Here that generation is blind, deaf, captive, prey, and spoil of the mighty. But in their helpless state, perhaps they are finally ready to hear God's word.

1. What attitudes do you see in the church today that are similar to those described in today's lesson?

2. What things could Isaiah have said that would make him acceptable to his generation?

3. Why is attempting to make God bless us through our religious behavior so attractive to us? What is the alternative?

FIVE

But Now . . .

Isaiah 43:1–7 *But now thus says the LORD, he who created you, O Jacob, he who formed you, O Israel: Do not fear, for I have redeemed you; I have called you by name, you are mine. ²When you pass through the waters, I will be with you; and through the rivers, they shall not overwhelm you; when you walk through fire you shall not be burned, and the flame shall not consume you. ³For I am the LORD your God, the Holy One of Israel, your Savior. I give Egypt as your ransom, Ethiopia and Seba in exchange for you. ⁴Because you are precious in my sight, and honored, and I love you, I give people in return for you, nations in exchange for your life. ⁵Do not fear, for I am with you; I will bring your offspring from the east, and from the west I will gather you; ⁶I will say to the north, "Give them up," and to the south, "Do not withhold; bring my sons from far away and my daughters from the end of the earth—⁷everyone who is called by my name, whom I created for my glory, whom I formed and made."*

Understanding the Word. So imagine that you are Yahweh. Here are these people who are supposed to be your servant, but are actually deaf and blind and helpless (42:18–22). What are you going to do with them? I am afraid that if I were he, I would just forget them and go looking for another servant. Would you rest your reputation in a court case with the gods on these people? I surely don't think I would. But that just shows we are not Yahweh, doesn't it? The disjunctive "But" that heads our passage tells the story. The people, and indeed you and I, have chosen through our rejection of God's Torah (his divine instructions) to become blind and deaf and are now experiencing the captivity to Babylon, and to sin, that stems from that behavior. *But now—our*

Creator, the Holy One of Israel, our Savior, looks right past that, and comes to us with love in his eyes and forgiveness in his hands. Who can believe a God like this? And yet that is exactly who he is, and what he does. It is our enemy who whispers to us, *Oh, he could never forgive you, not after what you have done and done and done.* That is not God! As Paul says, nothing (outside of our own will) can separate us from the love of God (Rom. 8:31–39). God is forever *for* us. That is what this passage is saying.

How much does God love his people? Enough to make a deal with Cyrus the Persian emperor (vv. 3–4). For more than four hundred years, rulers of Mesopotamia (Assyria and Babylon, where modern Iraq is) looked lustfully toward Egypt. That great ancient culture was a source of incredible wealth, and the Mesopotamians wanted it. This is why they had to take Canaan, where Israel and eight other small nations were: the route to Egypt lay through it. But although both Assyria and Babylon were able to conquer Egypt temporarily, they had neither one been able to keep hold of it. Now, Yahweh says, in return for allowing his people to return home and rebuild, he is going to allow Cyrus to fulfill the ancient dream. He is going to give Cyrus, and the Persian Empire, permission to hold Egypt fast.

As I said earlier, one of the fears about exile was of your people ceasing to exist as a separate people group. Parents would see their children become more and more acculturated to the conqueror's culture, losing their own distinct identity. Here (vv. 5–7) God promises that will not be the case with Israel. Her children will remain Israelites and will be restored to their land from every corner of the earth. Ever since the Roman dispersion of the Jews from Judea in AD 135, these promises have continued to resonate among the Jewish people and to a significant extent account for the amazing reestablishment of the Jewish state, which was the end result of a process of return beginning in the late nineteenth century.

1. Why is it hard for us to believe that God really does love us?

2. Do you think it was fair for God to "give" Egypt to Cyrus (vv. 3–4)? Why or why not?

3. How can we prevent our children from becoming acculturated to the "pagan empire" in which we live?

COMMENTARY NOTES

This section opens up to us one of the issues in this part of the book of Isaiah. That issue has to do with the identity of the servant or servants presented to us in these chapters. First of all, there is the issue of whether there is one servant or two. Some would argue that there is only one, and it is the nation of Israel. The problem with this position is that the servant is clearly seen from two very different perspectives, a situation that is apparent in the material selected for this week's lesson. On the one hand, the servant described in 41:8–16 (last week) was clearly in need of encouragement and deliverance. But the servant described in 42:1–9 is described very differently. This servant is confident in God, and in the mission given to him: namely, to bring God's divine order, or justice (see the discussion on "justice" that follows) into the world (42:4). There is no mention of this servant being delivered, but rather of his delivering others (42:7). Those who are convinced that there is only one servant would say that these are merely two pictures of Israel, before and after, as it were. One argument in support of this view is that this delivering servant is described again in 49:1–12, and in 49:3 is called "Israel." However, there is an explanation for that, which will be discussed in Week Nine.

Interestingly, this (42:1–9) is the only occurrence of the delivering servant in chapters 41–48. All the rest of the descriptions, which are clearly referring to the nation, are to the captive servant. In chapters 49–55 the situation is reversed, with only one of the descriptions being of the captive servant, and the rest to the delivering servant.

In fact, there is little doubt among scholars that two different servants are being described. The differences between them are so pronounced, as will be discussed in the daily lessons, that without prejudgment on the issue, it is hard to conclude otherwise. However, this raises the second issue: Who is the delivering servant? Here there is great divergence among contemporary scholars. In the past most commentators concluded that the reference is to Christ, especially on the basis of 52:13–53:12, which seem to have so many elements paralleled in the life of Christ. But many recent commentators, skeptical of the possibility of a prediction of someone hundreds of years in the future from the writer, have dismissed that possibility. But if it is not Christ being described, then who is it? Here there is no consensus. The language used to describe the servant is so universal in chapters 42 and 49, and yet so individual in chapters 50 and 53, that it is difficult to find a human being who could fit both. Yet it seems clear that a single individual is being described. As I will try to make clear in the lessons, I believe that if we did not know of Jesus Christ, we would have to posit someone very like him to satisfy the requirements of the descriptions of the delivering servant.

The delivering servant is said to bring "justice" to the nations (42:3–4). While the legal equity that characterizes the English term "justice" is certainly a part of the Hebrew concept, that concept is much larger than merely "justice." The Hebrew word is *mishpat*, which is also frequently translated "judgment." But it can also be translated "plan," "custom," "way of life," and "regulation." What do all of those have in common? They speak of a prescribed order or pattern. Many kings in the ancient world claimed to restore "justice" to their kingdoms when they came to power. The implication is that the predecessors had allowed things to fall into disorder, which the new man had to repair. Here it is not merely a kingdom, but the world that is in disorder. The world is indeed in a deeply disordered state, in nature, but especially in humanity. God's *mishpat* is the divine order for life as the Creator intended it to be. That, of course, includes legal equity, but it includes so much more. This servant will restore God's order to the world. No longer will the disorder consequent on sin prevail when this servant does his work. In 49:6 it is said that he will bring God's light and his salvation to the nations. That is another way of making the same point: this servant will come to a world sunk in darkness and oppression and will restore God's divine order.

In 42:24–25, Isaiah makes an important point about God's ability to deliver his people from the exile. If Babylon had indeed taken his people out of his hand against his will, then it could be asked how he could possibly take them back again, being no more powerful now than he was when they were taken from him. But Isaiah asks the rhetorical question, "Who gave up Jacob to the spoiler?" (42:24) and then immediately answers it with, "Was it not the LORD, against whom we have sinned?" In other words, nobody took God's people out of his hands. He *gave* them into the hands of the Babylonians in punishment for their sins. That being so, having given them up, he can certainly take them back again if he chooses, as 43:1–7 asserts he is about to do.

Another term that occurs frequently in this part of the book is "righteousness," a translation for two related Hebrew words: *tsedeq* and *tsedaqah*. Once again (as with *mishpat*, discussed earlier), this is not an incorrect translation, but it may obscure the central idea somewhat. Broadly, the words refer to "doing the right thing" in any given circumstance. "Righteousness" appears in this week's material in 42:6 and 42:21. So in verse 6 Yahweh asserts that calling this servant was the "right" thing to do. In verse 21 he says that he made his Torah—or "teaching," as the NRSV renders it—great as a way of demonstrating how right he is in all his actions.

But these terms are used in a special way in this section (chaps. 49–55) and sometimes in the following (chaps. 56–66) that the translations sometimes do not represent very clearly. Very often in these chapters, God's deliverance of his people is said to be an expression of his righteousness, his character of doing what is right. Was he "right" to send them into exile? Absolutely! He could have rightly done so hundreds of years earlier, but he patiently waited, hoping for a repentance that never came.

But would God have been "right" to leave them in captivity? From one point of view, one could certainly say yes. They had been told that if they continued in sin, they would "perish from the land" (Deut. 4:26). But actually it would not be right for *this God* to leave them there, for this God is a God whose faithfulness ("truth") reaches to the heavens. As the old Communion ritual has it, his "property is always to have mercy" (the Prayer of Humble Access).

So in many cases in these chapters, his "righteousness" is his saving grace. But here is where the translation problem arises. In these cases, many translations (including the NRSV) will translate with "salvation," or a similar word, where the Hebrew text actually says "righteousness." An example of this occurred in last week's lesson, in 41:10. The Hebrew says, "I will uphold you with my righteous right hand," whereas the NRSV says ". . . with my victorious right hand." Something gets lost in translation there. The Hebrew says that we can trust that God's great power (his "right hand") will *always* be used for what is right. "Victorious" misses that important nuance. I will point out other examples in later lessons.

WEEK THREE

GATHERING DISCUSSION OUTLINE

A. Open session in prayer.

B. View video for this week's readings.

C. What general impressions and thoughts do you have after considering the video and reading the daily writings on these scriptures?

D. Discuss questions selected from the daily readings.

1. **KEY OBSERVATION:** The character of the delivering servant offers a model for us.

   DISCUSSION QUESTION: What is it about these characteristics that makes them especially appropriate for Christians? Why?

2. **KEY OBSERVATION:** Since Yahweh is the transcendent Creator, he can do things that have not happened before.

   DISCUSSION QUESTION: How is salvation in Christ an expression of God's ability to do something new?

3. **KEY OBSERVATION:** God is impatient to deliver us from all the things that hold us captive.

   DISCUSSION QUESTION: What are some examples of things that hold us captive? Why does God not deliver us from them?

4. **KEY OBSERVATION:** The people became blind and deaf because they treated Yahweh in pagan ways.

   DISCUSSION QUESTION: What are some of the ways Christians treat Yahweh in pagan ways? How should we treat him?

5. **KEY OBSERVATION:** God loves us in spite of our sin and helplessness.

   DISCUSSION QUESTION: Why is it so difficult for us to accept (to feel it in a deep way) that God loves us in spite of everything we are and have done?

E. What facts and information presented in the commentary portion of the lesson help you understand the weekly scripture?

F. Close session with prayer.

WEEK FOUR

Isaiah 43:8–13, 16–28; 44:1–8

You Are My Witnesses

INTRODUCTION

Until this point we have not really been told in what way Israel, though blind and deaf, will be able to serve Yahweh, the one who has chosen them. That question is answered in the passage for this week. They will be his witnesses (43:10, 12; 44:8). But witnesses to what? That question is answered in 43:8–13. They are to be Yahweh's witnesses in his continuing court case against the idols. He calls for the idols to bring their witnesses who can give convincing proof that they are indeed worthy of the title "god." And then he calls on his people, who will testify out of their own experience with Yahweh. What will their evidence consist of? They will testify that their God did specifically predict both their exile, in advance, *and* their deliverance by the specifically named Cyrus, and that against all the odds, and their expectations, these very things had happened. In the end, their delivered condition will be the evidence that God stands outside of time—in fact, created time—and not only knows the future, but can do radically new things (43:16–21). Among those new things will be the complete blotting out of their transgressions (vv. 22–28), and the anointing of their children with the Spirit. As a result, their descendants will gladly identify themselves as members of the nation of Israel and exclusive possessions of Yahweh (44:1–8). In this passage God continues to offer encouragement (the base meaning of the Old English "comfort," Isa. 40:1) to his fearful servant Israel. He adds two more reasons why they should not be afraid: he will pour his spirit on their offspring (44:2–3), and in spite of all their flaws and failings—indeed, their sins—he will make them the living evidence that he alone is God. They will be his witnesses (44:8).

ONE

Besides Me There Is No Savior

Isaiah 43:8–13 *Bring forth the people who are blind, yet have eyes, who are deaf, yet have ears! ⁹Let all the nations gather together, and let the peoples assemble. Who among them declared this, and foretold to us the former things? Let them bring their witnesses to justify them, and let them hear and say, "It is true." ¹⁰You are my witnesses, says the* LORD, *and my servant whom I have chosen, so that you may know and believe me and understand that I am he. Before me no god was formed, nor shall there be any after me. ¹¹I, I am the* LORD, *and besides me there is no savior. ¹²I declared and saved and proclaimed, when there was no strange god among you; and you are my witnesses, says the* LORD. *¹³I am God, and also henceforth I am He; there is no one who can deliver from my hand; I work and who can hinder it?*

Understanding the Word. Here we have the second presentation of Yahweh's case against the idols. The first occurred in 41:21–29. There Yahweh asserted that there was no one who could come forward with evidence that their god had specifically foretold the future. Here that same point is made again, but taken further. God begins by calling the blind and deaf into court. It is not clear to whom that refers. It might be Israel, his servants, whom he called blind and deaf in 42:18–19. If so, what condescension on his part! Would he rest his case on the evidence of the blind and the deaf, people like you and me? In fact, that is exactly what he does again and again, touching our feeble efforts done in sincerity with his light and power. But another possibility is that he is speaking of the idols. Several times elsewhere in Scripture it is said that although the idols have eyes, they cannot see, and although they have ears, they cannot hear (see Psalm 115:5–6). This would be in keeping with his general dismissal of the gods' ability to do anything.

Now Yahweh specifically calls on the idols to bring forward witnesses who can say, "Yes, it is true. There was a time when my god made a specific prediction, and it happened." In fact, there would be no one who could do that (see the discussion on the idols' inability to tell the future in the commentary that follows). But God *could* call witnesses who could "justify" him (prove he was right). But he does not call them merely to give evidence. Look at 43:10–12.

God wants his witnesses to understand the meaning of what they have experienced. Why does he choose people like you and me to be his servants? Is it just so we can do something for him? No! He wants us to know him and believe and understand who he is. In Isaiah 1:3, Yahweh, speaking in Isaiah's own day, lamented that that was not the case. The people did not know; they did not understand. They apparently could not reason as well as a donkey or an ox could. What should their experience of God (and ours) have taught them (and us)? It is that there is only one God, one Creator, and therefore only one Savior. Too often we Christians, in a desire to be tolerant, sell out the truth of the gospel. There are not many ways to heaven, but only one: faith in Jesus Christ, his atoning death, and his resurrected life (see Acts 4:11–12). Can we confidently leave the fate of those who have never heard in God's just hands? Certainly, but that does not change the facts of what God has "declared" and "proclaimed" (Isa. 43:12). As we are told in 1 John 5:11, God has testified that eternal life is in his Son. When we have personally experienced that life, we are in a position to give convincing evidence that Yahweh is God and there is no other.

1. What is the difference between explaining the plan of salvation and being a witness?

2. What does it mean to "know and believe and understand" who God is?

3. Why is specific prediction of something that has never happened before impossible from the world's standpoint?

T W O

A New Thing

Isaiah 43:16–21 *Thus says the LORD, who makes a way in the sea, a path in the mighty waters, [17]who brings out chariot and horse, army and warrior; they lie down, they cannot rise, they are extinguished, quenched like a wick: [18]Do not remember the former things, or consider the things of old. [19]I am about to do a new thing; now it springs forth, do you not perceive it? I will make a way in the wilderness and rivers in the desert. [20]The wild animals will honor me, the jackals and the ostriches; for I give water in the wilderness, rivers in the desert, to give* *drink to my chosen people,* [21]*the people whom I formed for myself so that they might declare my praise.*

Understanding the Word. We humans do not like surprises. Oh yes, pleasant little surprises are all right, but genuine, out-of-the-blue surprises, not so much. The reason for this is that we are so fragile. We are fragile physically, emotionally, and spiritually. So all of us are control freaks to some extent. We want to be in control of ourselves and our environments so nothing unexpected or unforeseen will happen that might damage us or hurt us in some way. This is why paganism in one form or another is a perennial temptation for us. It promises us (falsely) that we can control the forces of the cosmos so as to maximize our comfort, pleasure, and security. Even we Christians want to do that with God. We want to be able to predict just what he will do in any given circumstance. But God doesn't operate that way; he is far too creative for that.

We can imagine that as the Israelites became convinced that God was indeed going to deliver them from Babylon, they had it all worked out. They knew how God delivers people from captivity; he had done it once before in their history. So God would choose a baby from among them; turn him into a great, if somewhat reluctant, leader; and they would cross the Euphrates River, dry-shod, while all the Babylonian armies drowned behind them.

When we look at verses 16 and 17, they seem to confirm all those expectations. They remind us of what God had done when he delivered his people from Egypt. But now look at verse 18: "Do not remember the former things." Why not? Because Yahweh is going to deliver them in a new way, a way he has not done before. This time, as will become clear later, he has decided that the deliverer will be a pagan who does not even know Yahweh's name. And he is going to take his people home, not by means of plagues, but by means of a royal decree. The newness of what he will do is possessed poetically: water in the desert; roads through the wilderness; and unclean animals honoring the holy God.

What is the point of this passage? Why did God remind them of what he had done in the exodus if he wanted them to forget it? It is just this: if God is never predictable, he is always consistent. What do I mean? We must remember what God has done in the past, because that teaches us who he is, and how dependable he is. But we must forget *what* he has done. The gods have to do everything the same all the time because they are part of the world.

50

In the northern hemisphere, the prevailing winds are always, sooner or later, going to come from the west. That's the way it is, and it is rather comforting. But God is not this world, and he will not do things the same way next time. Is he consistent and dependable in his character and his word? Oh yes, and that is something the gods will never be. They are simply humans writ large, and like us, they will trick and deceive their worshipers at the drop of a hat. Not Yahweh. What he does will always demonstrate his love and his faithfulness. How he does it? Hang on to your hat!

1. In the light of this passage, what does Jesus mean when he says of the Lord's Supper, "Do this in remembrance of me" (Luke 22:19)?

2. What are some ways we try to make God predictable?

3. What "new thing" has God done in your life?

THREE
I Will Not Remember Your Sins

Isaiah 43:22–28 *Yet you did not call upon me, O Jacob; but you have been weary of me, O Israel!* *[23]You have not brought me your sheep for burnt offerings, or honored me with your sacrifices. I have not burdened you with offerings, or wearied you with frankincense. [24]You have not bought me sweet cane with money, or satisfied me with the fat of your sacrifices. But you have burdened me with your sins; you have wearied me with your iniquities.*

[25]I, I am He who blots out your transgressions for my own sake, and I will not remember your sins. [26]Accuse me, let us go to trial; set forth your case, so that you may be proved right. [27]Your first ancestor sinned, and your interpreters transgressed against me. [28]Therefore I profaned the princes of the sanctuary, I delivered Jacob to utter destruction, and Israel to reviling.

Understanding the Word. In 43:21 God says that he chose his people "so that they might declare [his] praise," that is, testify to his uniqueness before the world. But in this passage, he says that, in fact, that is not what has happened. They have burdened him with their sins. Even though the biblical practices of sacrifice were quite similar to the practices of the Israelites' neighbors, the concept of sacrifice was intended to be very different. For the neighbors, the sacrificial system was a way of manipulating the gods. For instance, the sacrifices fed the gods; a well-fed god is a happy one, inclined to do what you want from him. On the other hand, if the god was evidently unhappy with you, you could magically substitute a sheep for yourself, and when you killed the sheep, the god would think you had died and would not be mad at you anymore. The biblical concept was quite different: God forgives us, as verse 25 says, "for [his] own sake." That is, he does not have to be manipulated with some magical ritual to make him do what he really doesn't want to. He longs to forgive us, and he had found the way whereby he can do that, while satisfying his justice (he tells us what that way is in Isaiah 52:13–53:12). The ritual is the human way of expressing gratitude and of demonstrating our obedient acceptance of all that he has done for us. Ritual is symbolic, not efficacious. That is, ritual does not change God. It is our way of physically representing our acceptance of what he has freely done for us in the spiritual realm.

What were the Israelites doing? They were worshiping in pagan ways. Instead of living lives that demonstrated that Yahweh is no idol, they were living unclean, sinful lives, and expecting their ritualistic worship to cover all that so they could continue to live in those ways. They were not worshiping and praising God with their sacrifices; they were just loading him down with their continuing sins.

This was what obviously concerned the apostle Paul in Romans 6, as well as virtually all his other letters. Were Christians going to use the sacrifice of Christ as a pagan ritual allowing them to continue to live God-dishonoring lives? God forbid! No, we receive God's free grace with joy, and demonstrate that we have received it with lives lived for God with love.

1. How are we Christians tempted to use ritual in pagan ways?

2. When God says he forgives us "for my own sake" (v. 25), what does he mean?

3. How does the phrase "let us continually offer a sacrifice of praise" (Heb. 13:15) relate to this passage?

FOUR

The Promise of the Spirit

Isaiah 44:1–5 *But now hear, O Jacob my servant, Israel whom I have chosen!* *²Thus says the* LORD *who made you, who formed you in the womb and will help you: Do not fear, O Jacob my servant, Jeshurun whom I have chosen. ³For I will pour water on the thirsty land, and streams on the dry ground; I will pour my spirit upon your descendants, and my blessing on your offspring. ⁴They shall spring up like a green tamarisk, like willows by flowing streams. ⁵This one will say, "I am the* LORD*'s," another will be called by the name of Jacob, yet another will write on the hand, "The* LORD*'s," and adopt the name of Israel.*

Understanding the Word. There are three important points to be recognized in this passage. They are: the gift of the Holy Spirit, the promise of descendants, and the work of the Spirit. In the passage we discover a fourth reason not to fear. We have already been told that we should not be afraid because Yahweh is with us, will help us, and will redeem us. Here we should not be afraid because God promises to pour out his Spirit on future Israelites. Why is the promise to pour out his Spirit an encouragement? It is because Old Testament believers increasingly recognized that they had a serious problem. That problem is nowhere more clearly articulated than in Romans 7:14–25, where Paul explains his inability to live the good life that God commands by relying on his own moral strength. The Jews recognized that all God's commands were good, but for some reason there is a stubborn resistance to them in the human heart. So they were afraid that maybe they were doomed to forever fall short of God's best. We can imagine that they were afraid that if they did get back home, it would still be the same story. But God promised that would not be the case forever. There would come a day, he said, when the Holy Spirit that they had seen enabling a Moses, or a Joshua, or a David, or a Micah to live wholeheartedly for God would be given to anyone who asked. Fear not! And, of course, that day has come. Jesus' death has made it possible for the sins that have defiled the temples of our lives to be washed away, so that the Holy Spirit can take up his residence in each of us (see Acts 2:32–33).

What does the Holy Spirit's residence in us mean? For one thing it means that we can have the assurance that we are truly the children of God. Very frequently in the letters of Paul, Peter, and John, we are told that the presence of the Holy Spirit in a person is the evidence that he or she belongs to God (see 2 Corinthians 1:22; Ephesians 1:13; 1 Peter 3:18; 1 John 3:24). That same point is made in this passage. The imagery is of someone tattooing the name of Yahweh on his or her hands. It is not merely the presence of the little box with a fragment of the Torah in it tied on the wrist that showed what one's commitments were (see Deuteronomy 6:8), but now it was the very name of the I AM that was present. That is all figurative, of course. Just as a little box of Torah could not make a person obedient, neither can a tattoo make one an exclusive possession of Yahweh. Something has to take place in the inner person for that exclusivity to become a fact. But that inner transformation is exactly what the Holy Spirit has come to do. He has come to make Yahweh the sole Lord of our lives, without a limit and without a rival.

As I have said several times previously, it is evident that one of the fears of the exiles was that they would disappear as a people because their children would be swallowed up into the Babylonian culture. God promises here that will not happen. The reason it would not happen was supernatural. It was not merely that the parents would do a good job of communicating the values of Israel, although one would hope they would do that. Nor was it because the parents somehow managed to isolate their children from the seductive elements of Babylonian culture. No, it was because God would be at work in those children's lives, bringing them to that place of exclusive commitment to him.

1. Why do we almost instinctively resist God's directions for living?

2. Why does allowing the Holy Spirit to fill us make it possible to live wholeheartedly for God?

3. What are some of the evidences of complete surrender to God in a person's life?

FIVE

The First and the Last

Isaiah 44:6–8 *Thus says the LORD, the King of Israel, and his Redeemer, the LORD of hosts: I am the first and I am the last; besides me there is no god. ⁷Who is like me? Let them proclaim it, let them declare and set it forth before me. Who has announced from of old the things to come? Let them tell us what is yet to be. ⁸Do not fear, or be afraid; have I not told you from of old and declared it? You are my witnesses! Is there any god besides me? There is no other rock; I know not one.*

Understanding the Word. This unit (43:8–44:8) closes as it began, with a reiteration (though brief) of Yahweh's case against the idols. Once more he declares that he is incomparable, that he is the only God, that he encompasses everything that a god could be, from beginning to end, that he alone has announced in advance what has actually come to pass, and that the Israelite people are witnesses to these facts. They went into exile in Babylon, as he predicted; they are about to be delivered by a man that Yahweh named far in advance even though nothing like that had ever happened before. So they are living evidence that Yahweh is who he says he is, the transcendent Creator of the universe, and thus the sole Redeemer of all who are in captivity, whether to other humans or to sin. The titles here are significant. Remember that "the LORD" is a stand-in for God's personal name, which is YHWH. (See the commentary that follows.) We do not know the vowels for certain, but they were probably *a* and *e*; thus the name would be Yahweh; "He Is." That would be his name when we talk about him. When he talks about himself, as he did to Moses, he calls himself, "I AM." As I mentioned earlier, this is to identify him as the one and only self-existent being in the universe. But he has chosen a people to identify with. Thus he is "the King of Israel." What that means is that it is very unwise to tamper with this King's people. At the same time, being the people of a King like that can be a very demanding relationship. He is not a fallible human king, and that is great news for those who trust him, but bad news for those who want to be in and out of the relationship, and to run their own lives from time to time. He is not going to tolerate that forever. But if we belong to this all-powerful, all-loving King, then we can know that he is not going to stand by and let the world hold his people captive. So, our

Source, our King, is the Redeemer, the divine embodiment of an institution enshrined in the Torah. If a member of an extended family falls into poverty, then his or her near relative is designated a "redeemer" (Lev. 25:23–25). That is good news for the poverty-stricken, but it lays a burden of responsibility on the redeemer. This entire part of the book of Isaiah tells us that the Holy One of Israel delights to carry that burden of responsibility. Finally, he is "Yahweh of Hosts." "Hosts" here refers to the angelic armies of heaven. God has all the hosts of heaven at his beck and call, as Jacob realized in his famous dream (Gen. 28:10–17). This is also what Jesus was referring to when he told Peter to put his sword away, because if Jesus wanted to escape what was facing him, he would not have to depend on one puny sword, but could call twelve legions of angels to deliver him (Matt. 26:53). It is clear what identity Jesus was claiming for himself. Yahweh will deliver his people, and there is no power on earth or in heaven that can stop him. Here then is a fifth reason not to be afraid. We are his witnesses; we have experienced or will experience all the glorious delivering power of our King-Redeemer, Yahweh of heaven's armies. Fear not!

1. How has this study enlarged your understanding of what it means to be a witness?

2. What is necessary if we are to have anything to witness to?

3. What does it mean to you that Yahweh is your King?

COMMENTARY NOTES

The metaphors "blind" and/or "deaf" are one of the features that unite the various parts of the book of Isaiah. From the first occurrence in chapter 6, where Isaiah was commanded to preach a message that would blind the eyes, deafen the ears, and harden the hearts of his hearers, the actual words, as well as the general concept, recur frequently. They can be found in 29:18; 32:3; 35:5, 42:7, 16, 18–19, and finally in this week's passage. In many of these it is said that in the future the blind *will* see, and the deaf *will* hear, providing the basis for Charles Wesley's famous verse: "Hear Him, ye deaf, His praise, ye dumb, your loosened tongues employ, ye blind, behold your Savior come, and leap, ye lame, for joy" ("O for a Thousand Tongues," 1739). The concept involves one of the numerous reversals for which Scripture is famous. Those who are proud of their insights and sensitivity are actually blind and deaf, whereas those who humbly admit that they do not really know very much or perceive very much are actually those who will gain the most from God's revelation (see Isaiah 57:15; 1 Corinthians 10:12).

While Moses said as early as Deuteronomy 32:39 that there was no God but Yahweh, it seems clear that among the Israelites he was pretty much alone in this insight. At least by the Judges period, the existence of other gods seems to have been taken for granted (see Judges 6:10). In the time of Elijah, Baal, the Canaanite storm god, was even considered a potential candidate to take over Yahweh's place as god of Israel. Elijah demanded that the people choose one or the other, something that flew in the face of standard pagan understanding (1 Kings 18:21, 36, 39). But it falls to Isaiah to make the argument that those forces and spirits whom the peoples of the world have worshiped are not divine at all. He makes the point repeatedly in chapters 41–46, as here in 43:10 and 44:6. In modern America, we, with our fetish for "tolerance," are moving back toward the pagan understanding.

Isaiah 43:23–24 is capable of a couple of different interpretations. One is that during the Babylonian exile, the people would not have been able to give the sacrifices that were prescribed in the Pentateuch because they had no temple, and indeed were living in an unclean land. However, that interpretation does not fit well with the attitude toward ritual and sacrifice that is expressed elsewhere in the book (see especially 1:10–15; 66:3–4). Rather, it seems that the prophet is saying that the sacrifices the people offered were worthless because they were not accompanied by appropriate actions of repentance (see Acts 26:20). So instead of the sacrifices satisfying God that the people really were turning away from their sins and intending to live a new life, they actually burdened him with the realization that the people intended to go right on doing what they had been doing, believing that their rituals made it possible.

"Your first ancestor" in 43:27 is almost certainly a reference to Jacob, particularly in light of verse 28. At various points in Scripture, allusions are made to Jacob's less-than-illustrious record. (See, for instance, Hosea 12:2–4, 8–14 where Jacob's flight to Syria is associated with Ephraim's upcoming exile to the same area; see also Deuteronomy 26:5.) In Isaiah 43:28 the people are arguing that it was unjust of God to have given up Israel, the descendants of Jacob, to "utter destruction," and God responds that their record going all the way back to Jacob and the subsequent "interpreters" (that is, corrupt priests and false prophets), puts them in no position to place any charge of injustice upon God. So, if the "princes of the sanctuary" (the high priestly family) were "profaned," it was because they had already profaned the temple with their introduction of pagan practices into the temple (see Ezekiel 8:5–18). All this is to underline the point made in 43:25. If there is to be restoration for Israel, it will not be because they, or their ancestors, have in any way deserved it. Nor would it be because they have suffered enough and have therefore somehow "worked off" their punishment (as a narrow reading of 40:2 might suggest). No, the only way back to their land and back to unbroken fellowship with God would have to be through his unmerited grace. He would have to forgive them for his "own sake" (43:25).

The entire segment (43:22–28) underlines the important point that Israel's ultimate problem is not physical bondage, but their alienation from God

because of sin. If they could somehow be restored to their land without forgiveness and restoration to God, it would all have been a mockery. Finally, they were restored to the land because God forgave their sin and welcomed them back to himself. We Christians understand how that was possible, as Isaiah 53 explains. God forgave them and forgives us, not because of anything we have done, but simply because he cannot bear to leave them and us to our just desserts. For his own sake he forgives us.

In terms of idols, it is important for us to be clear on the charge that they cannot tell the future. Several commentators accuse Isaiah of making a false charge on that point. Certainly the gods did make predictions about the future. But Isaiah's point is that they could never make *specific* predictions that then actually came true. When we look at ancient and modern attempts to tell the future, we see the truth of this point. The predictions are all couched in ambiguities, so that whatever happened, it could be said that that was what had been predicted. These predictions were all based on the recurring patterns of this world, which were all the gods and their followers could see. But when Yahweh predicted something that had not happened before, like a return from exile by a Persian named Cyrus, that was something brand-new that could only have been predicted by Someone standing outside the circle of time. Furthermore, it would either happen or not happen, and that could be demonstrated.

In 43:10, 13 (also 46:4), God says, "I am he." The Greek translation of the Old Testament helps us understand what that phrase means. The Greek has *ego eimi*, "I am." What Yahweh is saying is that he alone is self-existent, not dependent on anything else for his existence. Every other being in the universe, including the so-called gods, is dependent on something outside itself. Not Yahweh. Thus, when Jesus said of himself *ego eimi*, "I am" (John 8:58; 18:5), the Jews of his day knew full well what he was claiming for himself: he and Yahweh are the same.

We do not know for certain how God's name was pronounced. That is because the Old Testament was first written only with consonants. By the time vowel marks were added (sometime around AD 500), the Jews felt it was irreverent to say God's personal name. So whenever the consonants of the name appear (*YHWH*), they put in the vowels of the word "lord" (*'adonai*), producing the composite *Yahowah*. This composite was never meant to be pronounced. The vowels were there to remind the reader to say "Lord." But in the AD 1500s, when Martin Luther and others were translating the Hebrew text into German, they did not know that this process had taken place. So they represented the name of God as the German "Jehovah." This was picked up by the King James Version, but later English versions have corrected the error and have "Lord."

WEEK FOUR

GATHERING DISCUSSION OUTLINE

A. Open session in prayer.

B. View video for this week's readings.

C. What general impressions and thoughts do you have after considering the video and reading the daily writings on these scriptures?

D. Discuss questions selected from the daily readings.

    1. **KEY OBSERVATION:** To be God's witness does not demand special abilities.

        DISCUSSION QUESTION: What is the nature of Christian witness? What has to happen to us if we are to be witnesses?

    2. **KEY OBSERVATION:** We need to remember what God's actions in the past tell us about his character, but forget how he carried out those actions.

        DISCUSSION QUESTION: What are some of the ways we tend to "enshrine" the way God supposedly has to do things?

    3. **KEY OBSERVATION:** We must not attempt to manipulate God through ritualistic worship.

        DISCUSSION QUESTION: What are some examples of ways in which we attempt to manipulate God?

4. **KEY OBSERVATION:** The Holy Spirit enables us to become exclusively devoted to God.

   DISCUSSION QUESTION: What are some of the evidences of complete surrender to God in a person's life? What might not be such evidence?

   5. **KEY OBSERVATION:** If Yahweh is our all-powerful King, then we can be confident of his power to redeem us from all kinds of captivity.

   DISCUSSION QUESTION: Why is it illogical to expect Yahweh to be our Redeemer if we will not allow him to be our King?

E. What facts and information presented in the commentary portion of the lesson help you understand the weekly scripture?

F. Close session with prayer.

WEEK FIVE

Isaiah 44:9–11, 14–18, 21–28; 45:1–8

I Am God; There Is No Other

INTRODUCTION

In this week's scripture several of the themes to which we were introduced earlier are repeated, and in several cases they are developed more fully. Included are the folly of worshiping gods that we have made ourselves, Yahweh's absolute uniqueness, his unique ability to tell the future, his determination to restore his people, and his remarkable ability to use someone who knows nothing about him to be the deliverer of his people; namely, the Persian emperor Cyrus. Throughout this discussion, the central point is that Yahweh is not to be identified with this world.

As I have said already, this concept, which perhaps does not seem so remarkable to any of us who have a passing acquaintance with the Bible, is in fact very remarkable. The great thinkers of the world, whether ancient or modern, have not been able to believe this. For them, this psycho-socio-physical cosmos is the sum total of all that exists. In short, this world is "god." There is nothing beyond this cosmos. This is the position of the modern evolutionist as well as the most primitive aborigine.

The Bible alone, and those systems of thought derived from it, insists this is not the case. This is why only those religions derived from the Bible—Christianity, Judaism, and Islam—prohibit the making of idols. To do so is to try to capture God in the forms of this world, and almost inevitably, to fall back into the false understanding of reality that this cosmos is all there is. On the surface, this struggle may seem to have little to do with you and me, but as we explore this passage of Scripture in the coming days, I will try to show you that it has great relevance for us today.

ONE

The Folly of Idolatry

Isaiah 44:9–11, 14–18 *All who make idols are nothing, and the things they delight in do not profit; their witnesses neither see nor know. And so they will be put to shame. [10]Who would fashion a god or cast an image that can do no good? [11]Look, all its devotees shall be put to shame; the artisans too are merely human. Let them all assemble, let them stand up; they shall be terrified, they shall all be put to shame. . . .*

[14]He cuts down cedars or chooses a holm tree or an oak and lets it grow strong among the trees of the forest. He plants a cedar and the rain nourishes it. [15]Then it can be used as fuel. Part of it he takes and warms himself; he kindles a fire and bakes bread. Then he makes a god and worships it, makes it a carved image and bows down before it. [16]Half of it he burns in the fire; over this half he roasts meat, eats it and is satisfied. He also warms himself and says, "Ah, I am warm, I can feel the fire!" [17]The rest of it he makes into a god, his idol, bows down to it and worships it; he prays to it and says, "Save me, for you are my god!"

[18]They do not know, nor do they comprehend; for their eyes are shut, so that they cannot see, and their minds as well, so that they cannot understand.

Understanding the Word. In this passage Isaiah give us his most fully developed thought on the futility and the sin of idol making. He expresses this careful thought in the most biting sarcasm. This is so because he understands idolatry to not merely be wrong, but to be contrary to the nature of reality. That means that the person who engages in it is condemning himself or herself to a life of futility—of missed opportunities.

In verses 9–11 the prophet makes the point that the idols, being human-made, can do nothing. As a result, those who depend on them will constantly be disgraced ("put to shame"). What they put their trust in will fail them. Isaiah is hammering that point home, saying it three different times in three verses. This is in contrast to Yahweh, who is true to his word and will never disgrace those who put their trust in him (see Psalm 119:6, 31, 46, 80, 116; Isaiah 45:17; 49:23; 50:7; Romans 9:33). This is the point of relevance for us in the modern world. We may not make statues and call them "God," but again and again we put our trust in this world, and in man-made things, and in ideas solely

63

derived from this world. The result is that, as Isaiah says, we make ourselves "nothing." That is, there is no ultimate meaning in our lives beyond ourselves, and when life falls in upon us in tragedy or financial reverses, or abandonment, we have nothing to fall back on. (See the commentary that follows for further discussion of this thought.)

Isaiah mocks the making of idols in two different pictures. In the first, in verses 12–13, he speaks of the hard human work to create this worthless thing in human form. In the second, in verses 14–20, he makes the point even more tellingly with its great detail. He describes how a person plants a tree, and then cuts it down when it is large enough. One half of the log he uses for himself for firewood. But the other half of *the same log* he makes into an idol! Who cannot see the stupidity of such a thing? says the prophet. Cook your supper with one half, and worship the other?! Yet, like them, our minds are often darkened, and we do not see the silliness of our false trusts. We do so because the thought of entrusting our needs to one who cannot be manipulated or controlled and can only be trusted is just too frightening.

1. What are some ways in which we put our trust in this world instead of God?

2. Why does trying to find meaning in this world alone result in futility?

3. In what ways does committing your life to the transcendent God give meaning to your life?

T W O

I Have Redeemed You

Isaiah 44:21–23 *Remember these things, O Jacob, and Israel, for you are my servant; I formed you, you are my servant; O Israel, you will not be forgotten by me.* [22]*I have swept away your transgressions like a cloud, and your sins like mist; return to me, for I have redeemed you.*

[23]*Sing, O heavens, for the LORD has done it; shout, O depths of the earth; break forth into singing, O mountains, O forest, and every tree in it! For the LORD has redeemed Jacob, and will be glorified in Israel.*

Understanding the Word. This passage forms the conclusion to the previous section before we move onward to consider more fully what Yahweh intends to do in restoring Judah and Jerusalem through Cyrus. Thus, the things to remember (v. 21) are probably both what has been said since 42:13, and what God has done for them and said to them in previous years. The great danger in memory is that we so easily get it backward, especially when we are in difficulty. This is what happened to Israel in the Sinai desert (for one example among many, see Exodus 16:3). They remembered what they should have forgotten, and forgot what they should have remembered. When this happens, we can be sure that we will get it wrong. They should have remembered how hard their life had been, and how they cried out to God for relief (Exod. 1:14; 2:23). Furthermore, they should have remembered how graciously and powerfully God had delivered them from their bondage. But instead they forgot the hardships and the gracious deliverance, and remembered what, in fact, had never been the case.

Here God is calling on them to remember his predictive promises. If he had predicted that they would go into exile, he had also predicted that they would be delivered from that exile. They are also to remember their identity. If they had for a while become Yahweh's "enemies" (Isa. 1:24–25), that could not alter the fact that he had "formed" them to be his own "servant" (44:21). But along with these things, they ought to remember that in spite of their blind and deaf condition (42:18), Yahweh loved them still (43:4) and was going to use them as his witnesses (43:12). Furthermore, they should remember that as the transcendent Creator, he could do something that had never happened before: he could restore his people from exile (43:19). Furthermore, they should remember that Yahweh is the Redeemer, and that even the depth of their rebellion could not prevent him from finding a way to satisfy both his love and his justice and to forgive them (43:25). Finally, they should remember that he is no idol, and that those who trust in him will not be put to shame.

Notice that in the mind of God, their redemption has already taken place. In fact, the means of that redemption lay far in the future from the human perspective. But the transcendent one is not in time, so he can see past, present, and future together. In his mind, the work was already accomplished. (On the implications of human redemption for the natural world, see the commentary that follows.)

1. What have you remembered that you should have forgotten? How has your memory given a false coloration to those things?

2. What have you forgotten that you should be remembering?

3. What are some of the things Yahweh has redeemed you from, thus making you able to glorify him?

THREE
Yahweh's Uniqueness

Isaiah 44:24–28 *Thus says the LORD, your Redeemer, who formed you in the womb: I am the LORD, who made all things, who alone stretched out the heavens, who by myself spread out the earth; ²⁵who frustrates the omens of liars, and makes fools of diviners; who turns back the wise, and makes their knowledge foolish; ²⁶who confirms the word of his servant, and fulfills the prediction of his messengers; who says of Jerusalem, "It shall be inhabited," and of the cities of Judah, "They shall be rebuilt, and I will raise up their ruins"; ²⁷who says to the deep, "Be dry—I will dry up your rivers"; ²⁸who says of Cyrus, "He is my shepherd, and he shall carry out all my purpose"; and who says of Jerusalem, "It shall be rebuilt," and of the temple, "Your foundation shall be laid."*

Understanding the Word. These verses contain a remarkable brief description of Yahweh. They do it through a collection of participles. A participle is a timeless verb of action. You can recognize them here by the "who" clauses. The first one is in verse 24: "who formed you in the womb." There are then eight more of them. A well-known Old Testament scholar has built a whole book on Old Testament theology around this understanding: that God is known by what he does. That perspective, while not complete, is largely correct. The Old Testament contains virtually no philosophy of religion, and even less speculative philosophy. When you think about it, given who Yahweh is, that makes a lot of sense. If he really is transcendent, radically other than anything in his creation, how are we going to rationally explain who or what he is? That is the error of paganism: it tries to explain the divine by analogy with the creation. That is to say, "Well, the gods must be like us, only bigger." What you get from that is gods that are just humans on a grand scale, with all our good traits writ large, *but* all our terrible traits writ equally large. They offer no deliverance from those terrible traits, but just hopefully some mitigation of their worst effects from time to time.

What has Yahweh done? He has not even tried to explain his essence to us. We could never grasp it if he did. That is what Jesus meant when he said that no one but he alone, the same one who left heaven to be with us could reveal God to us (John 3:13). What God had to do was to insert himself into our life and show us who he is by acting in our world on our terms. In other words, the incarnation, Jesus taking on flesh, did not start with Jesus. Instead, Jesus is the culmination of what God had been doing from the very beginning.

So who is Yahweh? Isn't it interesting that the first thing he says is that he formed Israel, and us, in the womb? Before he says anything about creating the world in the rest of verse 24, he says that he gave life to his people. Why does he do that? There are a couple of possibilities. One is that this is a preliminary thought. Yahweh, their Redeemer, is the one who brought them into existence. Then we go on to explain just who this Yahweh is. That may be it, but there is a second, more intriguing possibility: that the basis of all his acts of creation was his desire to create other individuals like himself, in his image, who could experience the self-giving, self-denying fellowship that he knows in his own Trinitarian nature. The rest of creation is simply to make a home for us. In other words, the cosmos exists for us!

So he is the Creator. What else do we learn about him from his actions? He "frustrates" those who try to use sympathetic magic to figure out the future (v. 25), and "confirms" the predictions (v. 26) of those who have given up "trying to get a message" and have been willing just to enter his heart. He confirms those predictions even if they seem impossible, like drying up the sea. He is so powerful that he can even name the deliverer far in advance, and even make a deliverer of a pagan emperor who does not even know Yahweh. In short, the Creator of the universe, the Lover of humans, cannot be manipulated from within the cosmos, but he can break into it at any point to accomplish his saving will.

1. Make a list of the "who" clauses in this passage and think about what they mean for your life.

2. Besides the predictions directly related to the exile and the return, can you think of other Old Testament predictions that have been confirmed?

3. How has God acted in your life?

FOUR

Yahweh's Promises to Cyrus

Isaiah 45:1–4 *Thus says the LORD to his anointed, to Cyrus, whose right hand I have grasped to subdue nations before him and strip kings of their robes, to open doors before him—and the gates shall not be closed: ²I will go before you and level the mountains, I will break in pieces the doors of bronze and cut through the bars of iron, ³I will give you the treasures of darkness and riches hidden in secret places, so that you may know that it is I, the LORD, the God of Israel, who call you by your name. ⁴For the sake of my servant Jacob, and Israel my chosen, I call you by your name, I surname you, though you do not know me.*

Understanding the Word. Throughout this entire part of the book, from the first mention of the deliverer in 41:2, the descriptions of him have been becoming more explicit. Here they reach their climax. Not only is he named, but Yahweh speaks directly to him, amplifying the commission that was given to him in 44:28 to rebuild Jerusalem. One of the special features of this passage is the repetition of the first-person pronouns relating to Yahweh. The point of this repetition seems clear. Why does Cyrus surpass all the preceding conquerors in his ability to capture the known world? Is it because of his unique ability? Or perhaps it is because of the universal power of the Persian gods? In fact, it is neither of these, nor any other reason that would be merely derived from this world. Shockingly, it is because the God of this little captive group, the Judeans, has specifically "anointed" him. This is why the mighty Babylonian Empire would fall to him in little more than a year once he began to attack it directly. This is why he was able construct the largest empire the world had yet seen, stretching from the Aegean Sea all the way to India, and from Egypt to the Caucasus Mountains.

Verse 1's use of the word "anointed" is important because it is the same word that is transliterated as "messiah." It refers to the special oil that was poured on the head of a new king or priest, marking that person as specially chosen by God for the task to which he was assigned. Why is Cyrus to be the king of the world? Because the Holy One of Israel has set him apart for that task. It was not important that Cyrus had grasped the hand of the idol of Marduk of Babylon, as he did after his triumphal entry into Babylon. What was important was that Yahweh of Judea had grasped *his* hand (v. 1). Notice the verbs: I *go* before; (I) *level*; I *break* in pieces; (I) *cut* through; I *give* you. Can there be any question why Cyrus was victorious? It is simply because he is the servant of Yahweh.

It is so important for us to maintain this perspective on world history. Does God micromanage every person and every event like a puppeteer? Not at all. But he does constantly work through people and events to achieve his master strategy of saving the world. Nothing happens that is outside of his control, whether those acting know him or not.

Notice the importance of naming in verses 3 and 4. Cyrus may not have previously known the name of Yahweh, but Yahweh has known Cyrus's name, and in fact has given him the name he bears. I and others believe that the point here is that Yahweh told Isaiah the name of the deliverer 150 years in advance as the culminating proof that Yahweh can indeed specifically tell the future, which confirms that he alone transcends the time and space of the cosmos.

1. Think of some evidences in recent history that support the idea that Yahweh rules and overrules in human events. Perhaps you can think of some in your own life.

2. In the light of this lesson and the previous ones, why is it important that Yahweh can specifically tell the future?

3. What does it say about Yahweh that he can use a pagan person who does not know his name to accomplish his purposes?

FIVE

There Is No Other

Isaiah 45:5–8 *I am the* LORD, *and there is no other; besides me there is no god.
I arm you, though you do not know me, ⁶so that they may know, from the rising
of the sun and from the west, that there is no one besides me; I am the* LORD, *and
there is no other. ⁷I form light and create darkness, I make weal and create woe;
I the* LORD *do all these things.*

*⁸Shower, O heavens, from above, and let the skies rain down righteousness;
let the earth open, that salvation may spring up, and let it cause righteousness to
sprout up also; I the* LORD *have created it.*

Understanding the Word. These verses are the climax of Yahweh's declara-
tion to Cyrus. They are also a statement of the fullest implications thus far of
the contest with the idols. The language is reminiscent of Exodus, where the
plagues demonstrated Yahweh's absolute superiority over all that the Egyptians
called divine (Exod. 12:12; 18:11). God repeatedly asserted that "they" (the
Egyptians) and "you" (Israel) "shall know that I am the LORD [Yahweh]"
(Exod. 6:7; 7:5; 8:22, etc.) So we have it here in verses 5 and 6. What is the
meaning of that phrase, "I am the LORD [Yahweh]"? Everything in it is tied
up in the significance of the name. Yahweh calls himself *'Ehyeh* (Exod. 3:14)
which means "I AM," while the name he wishes to be called by is *Yahweh*, which
probably means "He Is." The point is that he is self-existent, the only being
in the universe that is so. And that being so, he is therefore the source of all
that exists in the universe. Thus "I am [Yahweh], and there is no other." That
is exactly right. If he is indeed "I AM" then there can be no other being of the
same order as he. Exodus 20:3 says that those in covenant with Yahweh must
have no other gods before him. Neither Yahweh nor Moses was interested in
a philosophical defense of monotheism with those former Egyptian slaves
at that point. What the commandment was enjoining was practical monotheism. It did not deny that there were things other people called gods, but
was insisting that for the Israelites, their covenant prohibited putting those
things on a par with Yahweh. Now the progress of revelation had reached the
point where it needed to be said that those humanly created concepts of the
divine did not even have the right to be called "gods." There is only one being

in the universe who has that right, and Cyrus was being given the responsibility and the privilege, whether he recognized it or not, of demonstrating that fact by doing something that had been predicted far in advance, but that had never happened before: sending the Judeans home from captivity and paying to rebuild their temple.

Verse 7 has created a problem for many people for many years because the King James Version gives the very literal translation: "I make peace, and create evil." There are two issues that must be addressed here. The first is a matter of correct translation, while the second is more conceptual. See the commentary that follows on the first matter, but let me say here that Yahweh does not create moral evil, nor does he cause people to commit sin. What is being said is that he is ultimately responsible for everything that occurs in the world. I emphasize *ultimately*. This is important because all pagan religions are essentially dualistic. That is, they explain evil in the world by positing that there is eternal good in the world and eternal evil, with each having equal power and authority. In this view, the two are in constant conflict, with one being in the ascendant for a while, and then the other. The Bible absolutely denies this. There is one God alone, no other. Therefore, if there is evil in the world, it must finally be because he permits it in the world as he has made it. Obviously, this discussion deserves much more space than we can give it here, but suffice it to say that the Bible holds that God intentionally made the world with the possibility that his creatures could do evil. He did that because we could not truly love him unless we had the real capability *not* to love him (i.e., do evil). It is in this sense only that he is ultimately responsible for the existence of evil in the world. He does not *make* anyone do evil.

1. When is popular Christian thought in danger of becoming dualistic?

2. How can God be responsible for the existence of evil in the world and yet not actually cause people to do evil?

3. We need to think about what we mean by evil. When is an outburst of nature evil and when is it not evil? Why?

COMMENTARY NOTES

Isaiah's statement that those who make idols are "nothing" (44:9) is much more profound than it might appear on the surface. The reason for this is that it reverses the biblical statement that God made humans in his own image. Idolatry makes god in the image of humans, not merely in form, but also in its understanding of deity as being analogous to humans. What this then does is make humanity the measure of all existence. But if humanity is the chief expression of being in the universe, then nothing means anything. For we are unable to provide meaning in ourselves. Thus Isaiah 2:22 says, "Turn away from mortals, who have only breath in their nostrils, for of what account are they?" The answer to the question is obvious: they are of no account! Death is as near as the next failed breath. This is what has happened to Western humanistic philosophy. Making humanity the measure of all things, we have ended up with complete meaninglessness. Indeed, those who make idols are nothing.

Isaiah 43:25 and 44:22 both speak of Israel's "transgressions," which God will "blot out" in the first instance and "sweep away" in the second. *Transgression* is the third of a trio of words that express our human alienation from God. The three are *sin, iniquity,* and *transgression.* There are several other words as well, but these three are the most common. Several times they appear together as something of a constellation of our wrong attitudes, condition, and relationship toward God. One example of this is found in Psalm 51:1–2.

Sin is the most general of these words. Like many other Hebrew terms, it is very concrete. It connotes an arrow missing its target. Thus, sin may be intentional or unintentional. God has set up a target for us by which we may shape our lives and behavior. But we have missed that target; sometimes it is because we wanted another target and sometimes it is in spite of our best efforts.

Iniquity is a now-archaic English word for which we have no modern equivalent. The Hebrew word from which it translates refers to an inner twistedness that can be both the cause of our sin and a result of it. In the latter case, *guilt* is a good translation. In the former case the word refers to that inner tendency to turn away from God and to our selfish desires. It is somewhat similar to what Paul calls "the flesh." We are not really responsible for this tendency, but it can be resisted and we become responsible when we refuse to resist it.

Transgression describes the most serious aspect of sin, for transgression is open, bare-faced refusal to do what God desires. Thus it can often be translated as "rebellion." In Numbers 15:30 it is seen as acting "high-handedly," that is, with a fist raised in defiance. In the book of Isaiah, Israel is frequently defined as children who "rebelled" (1:2; 66:24). Thus when God says that he will blot out or sweep away their transgressions, he is speaking of their most serious and deliberate sins, and saying that even these he has already forgiven.

When it is said that God has already forgiven Israel's transgressions, there are two factors to be considered. The first is that Yahweh is not constrained by time: the past, the present, and the future are all alike to him. Christ is not still to be crucified in the future from his point of view. It is in the present for him.

But there is another factor that must also be taken into account. This is called to our attention in 1 Peter 1:19–20, where we are told that Christ was destined for death before the foundation of the earth. This remarkable statement tells us that from the very inception of creation, there was in the mind of God the understanding that the creatures he was making could sin and that in such a case his holy presence would destroy them as fire destroys stubble. Knowing that, he went ahead with his creation, but was fully prepared in his own heart to take upon himself the full retribution for all that we would do to him, ourselves, and creation. Thus he could say to sinful, unrepentant creatures, "I have swept away your transgressions" (Isa. 44:22). It was done, whether they ever availed themselves of this greatest of all gifts or not.

Moving on, in 44:23, and again in 55:12–13, nature bursts into joyous song because of the wonderful news of Israel's redemption. This is an important point because at the opening of the book, heaven and earth were called upon to be witnesses in the case that God was bringing against his rebellious children: Israel (1:2, see also Jeremiah 2:12). This is a reference to Deuteronomy 4:26, where Moses called on heaven and earth to witness what was going to happen if Israel broke her covenant with God. The point is that nature obeys God implicitly in everything it does, and so the spectacle of God's human creatures rebelling against him is stunning. It is as though nature is saying, "If I can obey him, why can't you?" Thus, when Israel and the rest of us are redeemed from our self-imposed bondage, nature is relieved and rejoicing.

But there is a further point to be made here. This is particularly evident in the light of Paul's comments in the book of Romans. There he says that nature was marred in the human fall into sin (8:20). This point gains support from Genesis 3:17–18, where God says that the ground is cursed because of the sin of Adam and Eve. But the good news, according to Paul, is that in the final redemption of humanity, the earth will be delivered from this curse, what Paul calls its "bondage to decay" (Rom. 8:21). Thus what Isaiah is here describing is not merely metaphor. The mountains and the hills will rejoice in our salvation, because in our salvation is theirs too.

Next, looking again at Isaiah 45:7, remember that there are two issues to be dealt with if we are to correctly understand the statement, "I make weal and create woe" (NRSV), or "I make peace, and create evil" (KJV). I addressed the second, the conceptual one, in the lesson.

Now let me address the first, the one of translation. I said earlier that almost all Hebrew words have a very large pool of possible meanings. Where English might use five or six different words, the Hebrew would have just one containing all those potential meanings. This means that anyone reading the Hebrew text must be very alert to the surrounding context to get the correct meaning. In the statement under consideration, there are two such "loaded" words, words with a large pool of potential meanings. They are *shalom* and *ra'*. The first is often translated "peace," and the second "evil." However, the basic idea of *shalom* is "union." "Peace" is one derivative of that idea, but so is "wholeness," and even "health" or "well-being," (which is where the NRSV gets the archaic "weal"). Perhaps the best English equivalent for the base meaning of *ra'* is "bad," for the meanings of the Hebrew word can range all the way from "unfortunate" to "moral evil," just as the meanings of "bad" can. So what is being said here? It is being said that Yahweh is the sole origin of all things that happen, all the way from good fortune (*shalom*) to calamity (*ra'*). Without compromising human freedom and responsibility, nothing occurs that is outside of his good purposes. There is no other god who can do anything good or bad. He is God alone.

WEEK FIVE

GATHERING DISCUSSION OUTLINE

A. Open session in prayer.

B. View video for this week's readings.

C. What general impressions and thoughts do you have after considering the video and reading the daily writings on these scriptures?

D. Discuss questions selected from the daily readings.

    1. **KEY OBSERVATION:** Idolatry is an attempt to manipulate this world so as to supply our needs.

    DISCUSSION QUESTION: What are some ways in which we are tempted to trust the world rather than God?

    2. **KEY OBSERVATION:** We too easily remember what we should forget and forget what we should remember.

    DISCUSSION QUESTION: What are some of the things we should forget and what are some of the things we should remember?

    3. **KEY OBSERVATION:** The Bible characterizes God by his actions on our behalf in the world.

    DISCUSSION QUESTION: What can we say about God on the basis of the "who" clauses in Isaiah 44:24–28?

4. **KEY OBSERVATION:** Yahweh rules and overrules in history to accomplish his purposes.

   DISCUSSION QUESTION: What are some of the evidences of this truth in recent history? What is it about these events that point to divine action?

5. **KEY OBSERVATION:** God is *ultimately* responsible for all that happens in the universe. There is no competing evil power.

   DISCUSSION QUESTION: In what ways does popular Christian thought often succumb to a dualistic way of thinking? How should we combat this?

E. What facts and information presented in the commentary portion of the lesson help you understand the weekly scripture?

F. Close session with prayer.

WEEK SIX

Isaiah 45:9–13, 15–25; 46:1–13

The God Who Carries Us

INTRODUCTION

We come now to the final arguments in God's case against the idols, arguments that establish once and for all his desire, his ability, and his intention to deliver his people from their captivity. He begins by maintaining his right to use the pagan emperor Cyrus as deliverer (45:9–14). It is not clear whether Isaiah's hearers were actually objecting to this idea, or whether Yahweh is merely addressing such a possible concern, but he does so very forcefully, asking how a creature can question the Creator. Yahweh *is* the Creator and can do anything that is consistent with his own character. The next section (45:15–19) speaks to a concern raised by the previous point. Since he is constantly doing new things (like using a pagan as deliverer), it might appear that Yahweh is quite inconsistent, and that his purposes are hidden. He denies this categorically. If we cannot always predict *what* he will do, his purposes and his nature are completely transparent. Then we come to the final direct statement of the case (45:20–25). Here the focus is on the inability of the Babylonian gods to save their worshipers. Unable to predict the future, the gods are of this world, and being *of* the world, they are not able to save *from* the world. In contrast, the Creator of the world is not constrained by the limits of the world. He alone can break into it and deliver his creatures from whatever may happen in it. Isaiah 46:1–7 expands on this thought. The idol gods cannot save their worshipers, and in fact have to be saved by the worshipers, who carry them out of danger. In contrast, Yahweh carries his people from birth to old age. Finally, 46:8–13 sums up everything that has been said since chapter 41. It does so very concisely, yet powerfully. Israel ought to consider the facts and live in the confidence that deliverance is at hand.

ONE
Yahweh's Right to Use Cyrus

Isaiah 45:9–13 *Woe to you who strive with your Maker, earthen vessels with the potter! Does the clay say to the one who fashions it, "What are you making"? or "Your work has no handles"? ¹⁰Woe to anyone who says to a father, "What are you begetting?" or to a woman, "With what are you in labor?" ¹¹Thus says the LORD, the Holy One of Israel, and its Maker: Will you question me about my children, or command me concerning the work of my hands? ¹²I made the earth, and created humankind upon it; it was my hands that stretched out the heavens, and I commanded all their host. ¹³I have aroused Cyrus in righteousness, and I will make all his paths straight; he shall build my city and set my exiles free, not for price or reward, says the LORD of hosts.*

Understanding the Word. In these pungent words, Isaiah goes right to the heart of the issue: Who made whom? The repeated charge of Isaiah and all the other prophets is that to worship an idol god was to worship what your own hands (and even more, your own mind) have made. In a case like that, presumably you could correct the god, your own creation. But Yahweh insists that the reverse is the case here: he made us humans, and indeed, the whole cosmos, with *his* hands (vv. 11–12), and will we presume to tell him how to run his creation? Could a pot do that with the potter? Of course not. And neither can we tell the Maker of the universe what he can or cannot do. As we said earlier, this grows out of the question as to whether there is anything, or more to the biblical point, any*one*, beyond this cosmos. If there is not, then genuine newness is impossible. Everything will function the way it always has. In this case, the idea of using a pagan to deliver believers is absolutely new. How could that possibly happen? It had not happened before, and even more to the point, it seems to offend the normal rules of logic and propriety. Surely a believer should rescue a believer. Can the unclean rescue the clean? Perhaps it could be the other way around, but surely not this way.

But the one who transcends time and space ("the Holy One of Israel," v. 11), the one who made the cosmos, can do with it as he pleases, so long as that action is consistent with his own nature. And surely salvation is entirely consistent with his nature. So who are we creatures to question him about how he chooses to save us? In some ways this goes all the way back to Abraham in the book of Genesis. In Genesis 15, Abraham was told something quite stunning: that he and his wife, old and childless, would have more children than stars in heaven or sand on the seashore. Talk about a new thing! In many ways all creation held its breath at that moment. Adam and Eve, having fallen for the lie that God is untrustworthy, had not believed what God said, and the world was plunged into darkness. Now Abraham, having trusted God enough to leave his support system behind and venture into the unknown, is challenged to take the next step and believe God when he says something that is frankly impossible within the constraints of this world. But Abraham did believe God, and he was accounted as having done the right thing (v. 6). In fact, the only right thing a human can do is believe God. If we will not believe him, all the supposedly right things we might do are wrong, because they are founded on a lie.

This was the challenge for the Israelites in exile: Would they believe God? He promised to deliver them, but he was going to do it in a most unorthodox way. Would they believe God in spite of this "wrong" methodology? Again and again, God asks us to believe and do things that offend our rationality. I think he does that on purpose, precisely to stretch our trusting and believing capacities. God rules his creation; do we really believe it?

1. Has there been a time when God asked you to do something that really strained your understanding? Did you do it? How did it turn out?

2. Why is our right thinking and behavior wrong if we will not believe what God says about us and our condition?

3. What is shocking about the way God has chosen to save us from our sin?

TWO

I Did Not Speak in Secret

Isaiah 45:15–19 *Truly, you are a God who hides himself, O God of Israel, the Savior. ¹⁶All of them are put to shame and confounded, the makers of idols go in* *confusion together.* *¹⁷But Israel is saved by the* Lord *with everlasting salvation; you shall not be put to shame or confounded to all eternity.*

¹⁸For thus says the Lord, *who created the heavens (he is God!), who formed the earth and made it (he established it; he did not create it a chaos, he formed it to be inhabited!): I am the* Lord, *and there is no other. ¹⁹I did not speak in secret, in a land of darkness; I did not say to the offspring of Jacob, "Seek me in chaos." I the* Lord *speak the truth, I declare what is right.*

Understanding the Word. In this section we come again to the question of Yahweh's consistency versus his predictability. We tend to think, as apparently the Israelites did too, that the two concepts are synonymous. Unless someone is completely predictable, he or she is not consistent. So here, since Yahweh is so unpredictable as to use the pagan Cyrus, who does not even know Yahweh's name, he must be inconsistent. In other words, he "hides himself" (v. 15). But that is not the case at all. Whatever he does, unexpected as it may be, will always be consistent with his holy character. It is just the opposite with the gods of this world. They will be quite predictable (the sun god will always rise in the east; the storm god will always make his appearance in the west), but they cannot be trusted to care for their clients, or to treat them fairly. This is the point of verse 16. Those who trust in the gods of this world will be "confounded" because their gods will fail them: they will not consistently care for their people. On the other hand, Israel will never be "confounded" because Yahweh's care for them will be eternal (v. 17).

In support of that claim, Yahweh speaks of his role as Creator, that is, the one who is separate from his creation. As I have said in a previous lesson in this series, pagan "origin" (not "creation") stories around the world are built on the idea that matter has always existed in a chaotic, watery form. This does not necessarily mean that they were all borrowed from a single original, although that might be possible. Rather, all of them are working from the visible world and trying to explain ultimate reality on the basis of what we see. So, yes, matter seems to be indestructible, and water seems to be the basis of everything, and yes, while chaos will never naturally produce order, if order is not constantly attended to, it will very quickly degenerate into chaos. (For more on this, see the commentary that follows.) Why things are this way, and what it all means, is an unanswerable mystery.

So is Yahweh simply one more of the gods, emerging from chaos, attempting to manage chaos, but whose ways and purposes are finally hidden from us? To this, Yahweh answers with a strong, "No!" He did create this world on purpose; "he did not create it a chaos" (v. 18), but rather as a place for humans to live in. Furthermore, he did not leave his creatures in the dark about what he wanted from them and how he made them to live. He has explained it all in his revelation to "the offspring of Jacob" (v. 19). He has spoken what is "truth," and what is "right." Are his essence and his being far beyond our understanding? Of course they are; we are only creatures. But his *character* is absolutely clear, as are his purposes for us in creation. He has not spoken in secret (v. 19).

1. When something happens to us that we do not understand, all of us ask why. How is that a different question from the one being asked here? What *is* being asked here?

2. Think of four or five qualities of God that demonstrate his consistency. God is always . . .

3. What is mysterious about Yahweh, and what is not mysterious?

THREE
Yahweh: God of the Whole World

Isaiah 45:20–25 *Assemble yourselves and come together, draw near, you survivors of the nations! They have no knowledge—those who carry about their wooden idols, and keep on praying to a god that cannot save. ²¹Declare and present your case; let them take counsel together! Who told this long ago? Who declared it of old? Was it not I, the LORD? There is no other god besides me, a righteous God and a Savior; there is no one besides me.*

²²Turn to me and be saved, all the ends of the earth! For I am God, and there is no other. ²³By myself I have sworn, from my mouth has gone forth in righteousness a word that shall not return: "To me every knee shall bow, every tongue shall swear."

²⁴Only in the LORD, it shall be said of me, are righteousness and strength; all who were incensed against him shall come to him and be ashamed. ²⁵In the LORD all the offspring of Israel shall triumph and glory.

Understanding the Word. As I said in the introduction, in these verses we come to the final indictment of the gods. Building on what has been said in the previous arguments, Yahweh then goes on to the final implication of those arguments: he is the only Savior for the world. This is a strong statement, and it is troubling to some, but it is the inescapable conclusion of all that has been said to this point. (1) Because Yahweh is the one transcendent being in the universe, everything that exists is dependent on him. (2) Since he is transcendent, he created the cosmos as an entity separate from himself. The cosmos did not emerge from him, and the cosmos is not his body or a part of him. (3) Since he created the cosmos intentionally, he has a purpose for it. (4) Since he is separate from the cosmos, he sees its entire existence as a whole. (5) He can thus explain the past and reveal the future, all in the context of his purposes in creating the cosmos. (6) He has given humans the right to violate his purposes, with cosmic results. (7) He alone can deliver creation and the creatures in it from those results. The cosmos cannot save itself any more than a river can flow upstream. The gods, the spirit forces of the cosmos, cannot save themselves or any of those who bow down to them; only the one who is outside the cosmos can step into it and reverse its course.

These seven propositions are a rather technical way of trying to capsulize what this paragraph says more colorfully. Someone who expects a god he has to carry around to save him needs, from Isaiah's perspective, to have his head examined. That is simply silly. Yet, how easily you and I fall into that trap. We find ourselves trapped in destructive behavior, from something as obviously destructive as drugs or gambling, to something not so obvious, such as compulsive spending or a critical spirit, and we look to the devices or practices of this world to save us. It will not happen, as Alcoholics Anonymous has been demonstrating for many years. It takes Someone who is not of this world to deliver us *from* this world.

But Yahweh is not just Someone. He is the one and only God, like whom there is no other. That means that he is not only Israel's Savior; he is the world's Savior. That means that all of us have only two choices: either we confess our sin and turn to him in faith, or we are "incensed" (angry) at his claims of kingship over us (v. 24), and try to go our own way. But, in fact, both ways lead to the same place: "*every* knee shall bow" (v. 23, emphasis added; see also Philippians 2:10), either in adoration or in terror. The attitude with which we come to his throne is our choice; *whether* we will come to his throne is not.

1. Why is it not arrogant to say that there is only one way to be delivered from our earthly bondage?

2. Why aren't other gods as good as Yahweh?

3. Why does Yahweh's transcendence mean that there can be no other Savior?

FOUR

They Carry Their Gods; I Carry You

Isaiah 46:1–7 *Bel bows down, Nebo stoops, their idols are on beasts and cattle; these things you carry are loaded as burdens on weary animals.* *²They stoop, they bow down together; they cannot save the burden, but themselves go into captivity.*

³Listen to me, O house of Jacob, all the remnant of the house of Israel, who have been borne by me from your birth, carried from the womb; *⁴even to your old age I am he, even when you turn gray I will carry you. I have made, and I will bear; I will carry and will save.*

⁵To whom will you liken me and make me equal, and compare me, as though we were alike? *⁶Those who lavish gold from the purse, and weigh out silver in the scales—they hire a goldsmith, who makes it into a god; then they fall down and worship!* *⁷They lift it to their shoulders, they carry it, they set it in its place, and it stands there; it cannot move from its place. If one cries out to it, it does not answer or save anyone from trouble.*

Understanding the Word. This passage continues the thought of the previous one with one of Isaiah's trademark graphic illustrations. Can the idol gods save their worshipers? Of course not: the worshipers have to save the gods! The prophet paints a picture of the Babylonians going into captivity. We see them carrying their idols out of the temples and loading them onto oxcarts. The gods are such a heavy, heavy burden, as our twenty-first-century gods of image and position and uncontrolled desire are. Bel and Nebo are names of Babylonian gods (see the commentary that follows). The gods "stoop" and "bow," probably references to laying them down in the oxcarts. They are far from standing in their temples in holy isolation. Now the poor animals have to carry away these gods to whom the people have bowed down.

What a contrast, then, in verses 3 and 4. Yahweh does not need to be carried! In fact, he has carried his people even through all those centuries when the mass of them had at best presumed on his grace and at worst denied him. He carried them when they were helpless babies, and he will continue to carry them when they return to the helplessness of old age. Now only a remnant of the once-proud nation still exists. But they do not need to be afraid; he has not changed. As he has carried them in the past, he will continue to carry them in the future. Why would he not, for he has made them.

That being so, would they compare him to some idol god? Again, the prophet's skill with imagery is on display, emphasizing the contrast between the God who makes us humans and carries us and the gods who have been created and made by humans and have to be carried by them. It is so expensive to make our gods. We lavish our gold and silver on them; we hire professionals; we carry them around on our shoulders, and then have to nail them down to keep them from falling over. What will the future say about a culture that pays a man with a strong arm thirty million dollars a year, that idolizes him, and then has to make excuses for him when he turns out to be a thug and a rapist? Is it only chance that our Sundays are dedicated to this false worship? We have to carry our gods, when Yahweh longs to carry us. Is entertainment evil? Of course not. It is a God-given gift to us. But when it begins to take the place of the living God in our lives, then it has become a positive evil.

1. Think of some of the ways we are forced to carry our gods.

2. Think of some of the ways God has carried you.

3. If we are to experience God carrying us, what has to take place in our lives?

FIVE

The Only God

Isaiah 46:8–13 *Remember this and consider, recall it to mind, you transgressors, ⁹remember the former things of old; for I am God, and there is no other; I am God, and there is no one like me, ¹⁰declaring the end from the beginning and from ancient times things not yet done, saying, "My purpose shall stand, and I will fulfill my intention," ¹¹calling a bird of prey from the east, the man for* *my purpose from a far country. I have spoken, and I will bring it to pass; I have planned, and I will do it.*

¹²Listen to me, you stubborn of heart, you who are far from deliverance: ¹³I bring near my deliverance, it is not far off, and my salvation will not tarry; I will put salvation in Zion, for Israel my glory.

Understanding the Word. We come here to the conclusion of the entire argument that was introduced in chapter 40, and first fully stated in chapter 41. The question found its particular focus in whether Yahweh could deliver his people from Babylonian captivity. The point of the question was in Yahweh's identity. Is he one more of the gods of earth? Is he one more of our human creations to satisfy our search for meaning in our lives, and even more, for control of the forces that shape our lives? If so, there would seem to be no reason to think that he could deliver the Israelites from their bondage. After all, the gods of Babylon had evidently defeated him when the Babylonians destroyed Jerusalem, burned Solomon's temple, and carried the leadership into captivity, so what would have changed? In fact, Isaiah had argued that the Babylonian gods had not defeated Yahweh, that, in reality, he had predicted the event in advance, saying that the Babylonian armies were actually his agents of discipline (see, for example, Jeremiah 25:9; 27:6; 43:10).

Now, here, in conclusion the prophet calls upon his hearers in the exile to "remember" all that was said in the argument. He emphasizes four points. The first is that Yahweh is absolutely unique; there is no other like him. In fact, there *is* no other God at all. In our day, when tolerance has been elevated to become almost the only absolute, this statement is difficult for many of us to accept. Surely the gods of other cultures have an equal claim to a place at the divine table. But to us as well as to his ancient hearers, Isaiah says, "Remember [the argument for transcendence]." He does not enter into a complex philosophical argument, but bases his claim on one point: only a transcendent God could specifically predict the future. That ability says he is not a part of the universe, and that in turn requires that he be unique, since only one being can transcend all others.

The second point that Isaiah wants to lift up here is that Yahweh has done all that he has done out of an overarching plan and purpose. The gods have no other purpose than our human purpose: survival with a maximum of comfort, pleasure, and security, and that requires the amassing of power. Why are we this way? Because the gods are this way. Why are the gods this way? Because we are this way. Not so for Yahweh. He has made this world as a place for humans to live (45:18), where we might reach our full potential in the sharing of his character, and everything that he does is in relation to the fulfillment of that plan, including the use of the man "from the east" (v. 11) to deliver his people.

The third point is that Yahweh is absolutely dependable. What he has said, that he will do. Again, this is the very opposite of the gods, who are based in this world. One of the things we know in this world is that nothing is for certain. Predictable processes in the broad scheme of things, yes, but trustworthy, no. How especially is this true in the realm of human behavior. A missionary working with orphans in another culture said to me, "How do you convince someone of God's trustworthiness, when *every* trust they have ever had has failed them?" But if Yahweh has committed himself to something, it *will* happen.

The fourth point is to emphasize that none of this will happen because of the righteousness of the exiles. This point is obscured by the NRSV translation of verse 12, the latter part of which reads, "you who are far from deliverance." The Hebrew says, "you who are far from righteousness." "Righteousness" accords far better with the first part of the verse, "you stubborn of heart."

Yes, these people are God's chosen servants, but that is not because they have been so sensitive and obedient, and thus deserving of the salvation God promises to them. No, they have done nothing to deserve God's grace. Their role is to gladly testify when it comes that it had been predicted long in advance and has now been fully given, just as he promised.

1. How have you experienced God's faithfulness?

2. How does the concept of God's transcendence affect your life?

3. How do tolerance and a full commitment to Yahweh's being the only God go together?

COMMENTARY NOTES

In 43:3 we said that Yahweh was going to permit Cyrus, the Persian emperor, to conquer Egypt as a reward for restoring Israel from captivity. In 45:14 Yahweh, having been speaking of Cyrus, says that "the wealth of Egypt . . . shall come over to you," and we might think that the "you" is a reference to Cyrus. However, the conclusion of the verse says, "They will make supplication to you, saying 'God is with you alone.'" This argues that here Isaiah is speaking of restored Israel, in the same terms that he uses in 60:6, "[The nations] shall bring gold and frankincense, and shall proclaim the praise of the Lord." Some may ask precisely when that will occur, and conclude that it speaks of the millennial reign of Christ. That may be so, but in one sense it has already occurred and continues to occur, as the wealth of Christian nations has been poured into Jerusalem during the last twenty centuries.

Concerning origins, the Mesopotamian story of the origins of the world is the most complete of all of the pagan origin stories and provides a good example of the basic catalog of concepts found in almost all the origin stories in the ancient Near East. It may well have been the prototype for all the rest. I call them "origin stories" rather than "creation stories" because "creation" presupposes something brand-new coming into existence. That is the case in the Bible; it is not the case with the others.

In these stories matter has always existed in the form of a watery chaos monster. This female figure gives birth to the gods and goddesses, who then give birth to others. However, there are so many of them that they become very noisy and their mother determines to kill them. The gods, of course, are not in favor of this, and after various battles finally decide to have the god of wisdom to create a super-god, who is called Marduk. Marduk uses magic rites and weapons to kill the chaos monster and takes part of her body to make the heavens, where he places the gods. However, now that the gods are fixed in the heavens they have no way of providing food for themselves. So Marduk takes some of the blood of one of the monster's demon warriors and mixes it with mud to make humans who exist to feed and otherwise serve the gods. This is in the background of Yahweh's insistence that he did not make the world a chaos, but rather as a home for humans (45:18–19).

In terms of the transcendence of God, recall that I have mentioned the concept several times in these lessons. This is the idea that there is an entity that is not part of (transcends) the psycho-socio-physical cosmos. The Greek philosophers considered this idea, but finally rejected it as unworkable and fell back on the idea that there can be nothing that completely transcends the cosmos. Particularly, they insisted that if there were any such entity, it could not have personal qualities. Thus they were left, as are modern thinkers as well, with the idea that if there is any spiritual reality, it is found within the confines of the cosmos. That idea must lead to polytheism (many gods) because the cosmos is so diverse.

Yet here is the Old Testament which never entertains the thought that God is a part of the cosmos, but instead insists throughout that he, the personal God, is utterly separate from it. Where did the Old Testament writers get such a radical, unthinkable idea? When we ask them, they tell us that God told it to them. That is, he revealed it to them. To be sure, they learned it very slowly and very reluctantly, but he would not let up with them. They are very clear that they did not discover this idea because of their superior religious sensitivity (something nineteenth-century European Christian thinkers tried to attribute to them). Their answer makes perfect sense. If the greatest thinkers of the world could not come up with such an idea and hold to it consistently, how could a group of former Egyptian slaves do so. Revelation from the transcendent one is the only reasonable explanation for the appearance of this concept, and not only its appearance, but its pervasiveness in the Old Testament.

Monotheism is the natural deduction from transcendence. Only one entity can transcend all others, as only one entity can be the source of all others. Thus monotheism is obvious. But let transcendence go, as the modern West has done, and the immediate result is, as it has been, the appearance of a multitude of "gods." Along with this there has arisen,

of necessity, the insistence that one culture's "gods" are just as good as any other culture's gods, and all roads lead to righteousness.

The NRSV, following the RSV, has obscured the important concept of righteousness. In this lesson, it occurs in 46:12–13, but it also appears especially in chapter 62. This obscuring occurs when the Hebrew word for "righteousness" is translated with the English "deliverance." Why have the NRSV translators done this? It is because chapters 40–55 use the concept of God's righteousness in a somewhat distinctive way. That is, when Yahweh delivers his people, both from Babylonian captivity and from their alienation from him, these chapters say that this is an expression of his righteousness. They are saying that although it was entirely right for him to send his sinful people into captivity, it would not be right for him, being who he is, to leave them there.

So what is deliverance? It is an expression of Yahweh's characteristic of always doing the right thing. So, Isaiah 46:12–13 really says, "Listen to me, you stubborn of heart, you who are far from *righteousness,* I bring near my *righteousness,* it is not far off, and my salvation will not tarry." The important point here is that people are not far from deliverance, but from righteousness. They cannot save themselves by their righteousness, because they do not have any! Their only hope is that Yahweh will do what is right according to his own gracious nature and save them anyway.

WEEK SIX

GATHERING DISCUSSION OUTLINE

A. Open session in prayer.

B. View video for this week's readings.

C. What general impressions and thoughts do you have after considering the video and reading the daily writings on these scriptures?

D. Discuss questions selected from the daily readings.

1. **KEY OBSERVATION:** Many times it seems that what God asks of us does not make sense to us.

   DISCUSSION QUESTION: What are some possible reasons why God's acts and requests don't make sense to us?

2. **KEY OBSERVATION:** God is not predictable, but he is always consistent.

   DISCUSSION QUESTION: What are some of God's consistencies? God is always . . .

3. **KEY OBSERVATION:** Yahweh is God of the whole world.

   DISCUSSION QUESTION: Why is God, through Christ, the only Savior?

4. **KEY OBSERVATION:** A human-made religion becomes a great burden to its makers.

DISCUSSION QUESTION: What are some of the burdens that human religion imposes on us?

5. **KEY OBSERVATION:** There is no other God than Yahweh.

   DISCUSSION QUESTION: How can tolerance and an unswerving commitment to Yahweh's uniqueness go together?

E. What facts and information presented in the commentary portion of the lesson help you understand the weekly scripture?

F. Close session with prayer.

WEEK SEVEN

Isaiah 47

Babylon Judged

INTRODUCTION

With chapter 46, Yahweh's case against the idols, and his use of his chosen servant Israel to present evidence in that case, came to its close. The verdict was that the idol gods were not gods at all, that they had not conquered Yahweh to take his people into captivity, and that there was nothing the gods could do to prevent him from taking his people out of their hands and taking them home again. He alone is Lord of time and eternity, and history does his bidding, according to his eternal purposes in creation, and according to his plans along the way to accomplish those purposes. Now all that remains is to announce the implications of that verdict, first for Babylon (chap. 47) and then for Israel (chap. 48).

The implications for Babylon are cataclysmic. She had considered herself queen of the nations, without parallel in the world. That consideration was not without weight. In his visions Daniel saw Babylon as the golden kingdom. For much of the history of the ancient Near East, Babylon's region, southern Mesopotamia, where the Tigris and Euphrates came close together and then joined, had been the epicenter of culture. From Sumer (Shinar in the Bible), where most of the innovations that are now the foundations of human life, including writing and the wheel, first appear, to the kingdom of Hammurabi, stretching from the Persian Gulf to the Mediterranean Sea, and on into the time of Assyria, this region was the lodestar of culture, elegance, and sophistication.

But all that was to change. All of the wisdom and intelligence that had been poured into making the world a place amenable to human control had been in vain, because it had led the Babylonians away from the truth of reality, a reality they did not want to entertain, into a maze of darkness. As a result, Babylon was going to have to come down off her throne and sit in the dust. Her many gods would not be able to save her, and like those whom she had brutalized on her way to power, she, too, would be brutalized. The lesson for the modern world is no less poignant. We have used our great wisdom and intelligence to make humanity all-powerful. But where will the gods of human technology take us, if they lead us to believe that we do not need the transcendent Creator?

ONE
From the Throne to the Dust

Isaiah 47:1–4 *Come down and sit in the dust, virgin daughter Babylon! Sit on the ground without a throne, daughter Chaldea! For you shall no more be called tender and delicate. ²Take the millstones and grind meal, remove your veil, strip off your robe, uncover your legs, pass through the rivers. ³Your nakedness shall be uncovered, and your shame shall be seen. I will take vengeance, and I will spare no one. ⁴Our Redeemer—the LORD of hosts is his name—is the Holy One of Israel.*

Understanding the Word. Throughout the book of Isaiah, self-exaltation (pride) resulting in humiliation is an important theme. This is especially prominent in 2:6–22, which moves from the heights to the depths, and from fullness to emptiness. The larger section in which that passage appears, 2:6–4:1, closes with another picture that is very reminiscent of the one here in chapter 47. There in 3:16–4:1 the "daughters of Zion" are first depicted as very haughty in their elegant, expensive clothing and accessories. But in the end they are shown as desolate, despairing, and diseased. So here, too, the language has clearly been chosen to emphasize a similar dramatic contrast. On the one hand, there is the beautiful queen on her "throne," "tender and delicate," veiled off from common eyes, like an untouched flower. (As regards "virgin daughter," see the commentary that follows.) On the other hand, there is what the queen will become: a slave girl grinding grain by rolling one heavy stone over another, or washing clothes in the river, with her rags hitched up around her waist, shamefully baring herself to any who cared to stare at such an insignificant creature.

What is the point that Isaiah is seeking to make with this recurring theme? It is that human worth will never be realized by operating from a false premise at the outset. This goes all the way back to Genesis 11. There a profound point can easily be obscured in what appears on the surface to be a quaint legend. Questions about the historicity of the account, while important, are not my main concern here. Rather, I am interested in that profound point. We humans live with the fear of insignificance. ("[W]e shall be scattered abroad," v. 4). So how do we fight that fear? We try to make ourselves as permanent and as important as we can. ("[L]et us build . . . a city, and a tower," v. 4). But what was the result of their efforts? It was the precise thing they dreaded: they *were* scattered over the earth, with the added burden of differing languages. The narrative says that this outcome was the result of Yahweh's action, and I would suggest that this is still true, although his action now is indirect. God has made the world so that self-exaltation leads to humiliation. For the fact is that in ourselves we *are* insignificant, and all of our attempts to deny that fact will only finally underline it. In reality, only I AM is truly significant (glorious), and if, in our vain attempts to puff ourselves, we act as though that were not so, we have constructed a house on sand. If nothing else, death will put an end to all our posturing (see especially Isaiah 14:4–21).

On the other hand, if we begin with that premise that Yahweh alone is great and gladly join ourselves to him, the Redeemer, Yahweh of heaven's armies, the Holy One of Israel, we will discover with wonder that by being his, we share his eternal worth. We each become someone by our relationship to him who *is* Someone. Babylon made the bad mistake of assuming she was someone in herself.

1. The church has designated pride as the first of the seven deadly sins. Why do you think this is so?

2. Why do our attempts to make ourselves important necessarily lead to our humiliation?

3. What does the realization that Christ died for us mean for our self-worth?

TWO
You Did Not Lay These Things to Heart

Isaiah 47:5–7 *Sit in silence, and go into darkness, daughter Chaldea! For you shall no more be called the mistress of kingdoms.* *⁶I was angry with my people, I profaned my heritage; I gave them into your hand, you showed them no mercy; on the aged you made your yoke exceedingly heavy.* *⁷You said, "I shall be mistress forever," so that you did not lay these things to heart or remember their end.*

Understanding the Word. Isaiah says here that one of the worst effects of pride is that it makes us think we are not accountable for our actions. This is why one of the populations with the highest sense of self-worth is the criminal population. They consider themselves smarter and tougher than anybody else, so they don't have to work and they actually have a right to other people's stuff. How does the Old Testament define this problem? They lack "the fear of God." As I said earlier, this is not living in a constant state of dread that an unpredictable and inconsistent God will suddenly lash out and hurt me in some way. Neither is it living in continual anxiety that a gimlet-eyed Judge is intently watching to see if we make one misstep so he can "throw the book" at us. Rather, it is to recognize that we are responsible for our choices and that sooner or later a compassionate, but just, Father will hold us accountable for the results of those choices.

So God, at the end of a thousand years of patience, finally gave Babylon permission to attack and capture his people. However, that was not the way Babylon saw it. They, in their pride ("mistress forever," v. 7), were confident that they had accomplished all their various conquests as a result of their own power, and that that gave them the right to treat their captives however they wished, including mercilessly and without restraint.

But that was not the case. Babylon did not stand on the top of the heap, as it were. Whether they admitted it or not, there was someone above them. That someone was Yahweh, apparently the god of little Judah, but in fact, God of the whole world. Babylon was going to be called to account. This is much the same point that is made in the book of Habakkuk. There the prophet suggests that God is unjust to use the wicked Babylonians to punish his people, when his people are not really as bad as the Babylonians. Yahweh does not explain why he chose to do that, but he does say that the Babylonians will not escape judgment either. The moral law will be applied to them just as stringently as it was applied to his own people. None of us is ultimate; every one of us must remember that our actions will one day require an accounting. That should cause us to act a good deal more carefully than we often do.

1. How does pride make us think we "can get away with murder"?

2. What are some instances in your life when you would have acted differently if you had recognized that you were accountable for what you were choosing to do?

3. Sometimes, knowing a choice is wrong according to God, we say, "I know what I am doing, and I will take responsibility for it." What are some other reasons (beyond the effects on our own lives) why we should not do that?

THREE
Useless Defenses

Isaiah 47:8–9 *Now therefore hear this, you lover of pleasures, who sit securely, who say in your heart, "I am, and there is no one besides me; I shall not sit as a widow or know the loss of children"—⁹both these things shall come upon you in a moment, in one day: the loss of children and widowhood shall come upon you in full measure, in spite of your many sorceries and the great power of your enchantments.*

Understanding the Word. Given our human fragility, there are several things that we use to try to protect ourselves from unpleasant occurrences that might endanger us. At least four of those are mentioned here. They are pleasure, security, abundance, and control. To these we may add comfort, which might be suggested by the verb "sit" in verse 8. The Babylonians had all of these, or at least so they thought. This is what the apostle John is talking about in his description of "the world" in 1 John 2:16. He speaks of the desire of the flesh—pleasure; the desire of the eyes—possessions; and the pride of life—position and power. That is, he speaks of a life that is in bondage to desire.

Something tells us that if we had all that we desire, and the means to continue to supply our desires, we would be truly secure. But what we do not realize is that desire itself is purely temporary, that it is insatiable, and that it will quickly pass away. When we are eighteen years old, life seems to stretch before us endlessly. When we are seventy-eight, it is almost impossible to believe how quickly it has all passed. One of the most famous of the twentieth-century movie stars is supposed to have said on his deathbed, "I had no idea it would all go by so quickly." So if we build our lives on pleasure, comfort, and security, we have built on what cannot endure.

Here Babylon seems to have limitless funds to underwrite any pleasure she desires. When one of Nebuchadnezzar's wives longed for her native mountains, the king simply brought her mountains to her in the world-famous "hanging gardens." Babylon is like an endlessly fertile woman surrounded by her children, and who, with the presence of her husband, can produce as many more children as she might like. This figure seems odd to us in this day of overpopulation, but in Isaiah's day, such a woman was the envy of everyone, women and men alike. She had no cares at all, her children would provide for her into her old age, and in them, she would survive long after her death. But all that security was as flimsy as a breeze. In a moment her husband and all her children could be taken from her, and she would go from the most-envied person in the world to the most-pitied. So it is with all of us who depend on the changing winds of this world to supply all our desires and somehow make us secure.

1. What are some of the ways our culture panders to desire?

2. Buddhism suggests that the way to a peaceful life is to destroy desire. This is both unrealistic and unwise. How does the biblical understanding of life help us control our desires?

3. How does a Christian handle the transitory nature of desire?

FOUR

Your Knowledge Has Led You Astray

Isaiah 47:10–13 *You felt secure in your wickedness; you said, "No one sees me." Your wisdom and your knowledge led you astray, and you said in your heart, "I am, and there is no one besides me." ¹¹But evil shall come upon you, which you cannot charm away; disaster shall fall upon you, which you will not be able to ward off; and ruin shall come on you suddenly, of which you know nothing.*

¹²Stand fast in your enchantments and your many sorceries, with which you have labored from your youth; perhaps you may be able to succeed, perhaps you may inspire terror. ¹³You are wearied with your many consultations; let those who study the heavens stand up and save you, those who gaze at the stars, and at each new moon predict what shall befall you.

Understanding the Word. Verse 9 at the end of the previous paragraph, with its reference to "sorceries" and "enchantments," has already prepared us for the major content of this passage. The way the ancients sought to gain control of this dangerous cosmos was through sympathetic magic. That is, if something is done in the visible world, it is repeated in the invisible world. This is the principle of voodoo. For instance, I wish to kill an enemy without being convicted of murder. So I make a model of him, perhaps putting a fingernail clipping or a hair of his on the model. I will also say some ritual over it that is designed to ensure that the likeness and the man are indeed one and the same. Then something destructive is done to the model, and perhaps 51 percent of the time something very bad happens to my enemy.

This is the thought world of paganism. Obviously there are forces controlling this world that we cannot see. The question is how to get control of those forces. In an earlier lesson we talked about this worldview. The Babylonians had applied vast learning and energy to mastery of this worldview and even more to harnessing these ideas for their own use. So they kept careful track of all the omens that had ever occurred in the past and had these carefully cataloged in what ran to almost seventy volumes. Thus, if the liver of the sacrificial animal was in a certain shape, or if the stars were in a certain formation, it would be possible to know exactly (more or less!) what was going to happen. (For further discussion of this idea, see the commentary that follows.)

Isaiah says that their great learning and intellectual effort had only led them astray. They were so intelligent that they were able to manufacture ways of explaining the world that gave them the illusion of control. No wonder they were able to say with confidence what only the transcendent one, Yahweh, can say: "I am, and there is no one besides me" (v. 10). What an incredibly foolish thing for any creature to say. Of course we are not self-existent. And we are only one among billions of other created things in the cosmos. Yet in our vain attempts to give ourselves significance and permanence, how many of us live as if this obvious falsehood were true? Like the Babylonians, we use whatever rational skills we have to support what is finally a fatal illusion.

1. How are our obvious intellectual skills leading us Americans astray?

2. How is it possible for genuinely intelligent people who are seriously seeking truth (that which is *so*) to be quite wrong in their findings? Consider the implications of John 7:17 here.

3. If, whether I am aware of it or not, I actually believe "I am, and there is no one besides me," what will be some of the manifestations of that?

FIVE
No One to Save You

Isaiah 47:14–15 *See, they are like stubble, the fire consumes them; they cannot deliver themselves from the power of the flame. No coal for warming oneself is this, no fire to sit before!* [15]*Such to you are those with whom you have labored, who have trafficked with you from your youth; they all wander about in their own paths; there is no one to save you.*

Understanding the Word. One of the political realities of the ancient world, as well as of the modern one, was a pattern of overlapping treaty relations. Any one nation had covenants with several surrounding ones, even with nations that were enemies of each other. This was all secured, as much as it could be secured, with interlocking marriages. This was one of the reasons, beside simple male posturing, for the large harems that many kings maintained.

They contained the king's many "trophy wives," daughters of other kings, with whom their husbands had treaties.

This had been the means by which Babylon had finally brought down their age-old nemesis, the Assyrians. For hundreds of years the Babylonians had been under the thumb of their northern cousins, the Assyrians, whom the Babylonians considered to be barbarians. Several times Babylon had revolted, but the Assyrians had put down each revolt with vicious force. Finally, the Babylonians had gotten smart and had allied themselves with the Medes, a warlike people who lived in the mountains on what is now the border between Iraq and Iran, east of Assyria. With their combined strength the Medo-Babylonian alliance had defeated Assyria in little more than fifteen years. But now the "worm had turned"; the Medes had deserted their alliance with Babylon and allied themselves with Persia, whom they rightly judged to be the winners.

That is the picture here. Babylon had been certain that she had made herself secure in the spiritual realm with sorceries and enchantments (vv. 9, 12), but that had all failed (v. 11). In the political realm they thought they had made themselves secure through all their alliances. But now they were seeing that there is no security in human promises, especially if those promises were self-serving from the outset. It is not as though the whole shaky structure would collapse suddenly, says Isaiah. It would just slowly and irrevocably dissolve (v. 15). All the hard military, political, and diplomatic labor that had been put in since the first days of Nebuchadnezzar would simply melt away like a pat of butter in the noonday sun. All that effort to guarantee their security would be for nothing.

So it is with us. We in America have been spared the almost universal warfare that seems to characterize the human condition, but we can only wonder how long this gracious gift of God to our God-fearing ancestors will persist, given our systematic dismantling of our ancestors' faith. But even in our hothouse environment, if we are at all thoughtful, we know there is no security in the human devices of this world. Intellectual fashions come and go, and what was intellectual dogma a generation ago is now laughed at. We may carefully accumulate wealth only to see it vanish in a stock-market correction. We may stake our whole future on the promises of a loved one, only to see those promises trashed on a moment's whim. There is nothing in this world that can finally save us *from* this world. Only he who stands outside the world can reach in and deliver us from it.

1. Besides the examples already discussed, what are some other ways we are tempted to make ourselves secure in this world?

2. Exactly how are we secure in God? (Reflect on such passages as Psalm 27:9–10.)

3. Why is this world finally unable to give us security?

COMMENTARY NOTES

When John wrote his Apocalypse—the book of Revelation—he used Babylon to represent all the glories and evils of the world. But by the time John wrote, Babylon had been long eclipsed by Rome, and many scholars think that he was using "Babylon" as a code term for Rome. But why would he do that? The answer is that for some three thousand years of shining history, the region in which Babylon was located and which Babylon came to epitomize had represented all that is great in human achievement.

That region was southern Mesopotamia, where the Tigris and Euphrates Rivers, close together in the north and then again in the south, enclosed a kind of rough oval of about 150 miles north to south and about 75 miles east to west. Today the two rivers join together just south of the oval, but it is thought that the ancient coast of the Persian Gulf reached just north of that present joining. This oval was the home of the ancient Sumerians, a people whose origins we know little about, but who are responsible for almost all the basics of the human culture we take for granted, chief of which are the wheel and writing. Another invention of theirs was base 60 mathematics, from which we get the sixty-minute hour and the 360-degree circle. The list of their achievements could be expanded exponentially, but this is enough to give some sense of their brilliance.

Part of the reason for these achievements was the abundant irrigation water that the two rivers provided. This meant that an excess of food could be raised without an eighteen-hour day of incessant labor. This excess meant possibilities for trade but also the leisure to explore the truly human possibilities, such as literature, music, art, and architecture.

When the Sumerians were eventually displaced by people speaking Semitic language, these newcomers only increased the earlier glory. Eventually, about 1700 BC, the Semitic king Hammurabi established his capital near the northern edge of the oval at a place called *bab ili*, "gate of God." The Greek transliteration of that name had given us "Babylon." For the next fifteen hundred years, this city encapsulated all of the driving energy, the elegance, and the sophistication of which humanity at the peak of its powers is capable. For the people of the ancient world it was simply *the best*.

Looking now at this week's scripture passage, the phrase "virgin daughter" (47:1) is used to convey an image of that which is beautiful, delicate, and untouched. In Isaiah 37:22 the image is used of Jerusalem as she mocks the Assyrian emperor Sennacherib, who had thought to capture the city and plunder it. In fact, although Jerusalem was as helpless and vulnerable as a virgin daughter, the brutal conqueror would be able to do nothing to the city. So here it is used to highlight the contrast between Babylon as she thought herself to be and Babylon as she was to become.

"Chaldea" (47:1, 5), when used technically, refers to the extreme southern part of Mesopotamia. It was very marshy and difficult to travel through. The great Sumerian city of Ur was located just on the edge of this region, and so is called in the Bible "Ur of the Chaldeans" (Gen. 11:31). During the years of Assyrian oppression (ca. 900–525 BC), Babylonian rebels often hid in this area. Thus, when the city and the region gained its independence and defeated the Assyrians, the entire region of southern Mesopotamia began to be referred to as Chaldea.

The next important phrase, "profaned my heritage" in 47:6, is made somewhat obscure by the translation "heritage" or "inheritance." While the relevant Hebrew term can be correctly translated that way, that is not the only meaning of the term. In the broadest sense it refers to "a special possession." An inheritance is, of course, such a special possession, but the connotation is not limited to inheritance. So, on the one hand the land of Israel is referred to as the "inheritance" of the people of Israel (Num. 26:53). Here, the idea of property that is passed down from one generation to the next is quite appropriate. But what does it mean when the same Hebrew word is used of Israel in relation to God ("possession" in Deut. 4:20)? Is Israel the "inheritance" of God? How could that work? Who did God inherit from? The point is, of course, that just as the land is "the special possession" of the people of Israel, so Israel is "the special possession" of Yahweh.

But what does it mean for Yahweh to "profane" his special possession? When we think of "profane," we tend to give it religious overtones. But that is not always the case in the Old Testament. To profane something can mean as little as treating something commonly. That is the sense being used here. Yahweh is no longer treating his special possession as special anymore. He has dropped it on the ground and allowed the animals to walk on it. However, he did not intend that the animals would chew it up and throw it around, as they have done, and they will be held accountable for that.

Now we will move on to our final emphasis for this week. In an earlier lesson I spoke briefly about the prominence of omens in the attempts by Israel's neighbors to predict the future. It is appropriate to say more about that practice in the context of the references in this chapter. Omenology is rooted squarely in that understanding of reality cosmos that is typical of pagan thought. I have labeled this understanding as "continuity." It is the opposite of transcendence. Transcendence says God is *not* continuous with the cosmos, that there is a radical distinction between the Creator and the creation. Furthermore, each element of creation—for instance, humanity and nature—is distinct from the other. Continuity argues the very opposite: there is nothing beyond the cosmos. Thus the gods are continuous with the cosmos. Furthermore, everything in the cosmos is continuous with everything else in the cosmos; touch one part of it and you touch the whole.

How does this explain omenology? On this understanding existence is one endless cycle. Whatever has happened will happen again, and whatever is happening has happened before. This is the basis for the idea of reincarnation. The past, the present, and the future are all continuous with each other. Thus, whatever happened in the past when the stars were in a certain configuration will necessarily happen again when the stars are in that configuration again. In the same way, if something happened in the past when the sacrificial animal's liver was in a certain shape, then that will happen again whenever the sheep's liver is that same shape.

Of course, it took immense effort to record, refine, organize, and catalog all that data over the centuries. Furthermore, it took incredible abilities of recall to know what a given sign, or omen, might mean. (Not to mention a very facile mind to know how to "massage" the data so as not to displease the royal client!)

All of this was for the purpose of control. The concept of continuity gives the illusion that we can control the complex cosmos around us by manipulating one part and getting the result we want in another. Tragically, it is just that, an illusion.

Our culture does not prescribe to continuity in the way that the ancients did, but our determination to gain control of our environment in order to make ourselves secure is no less passionate, and no less misguided. Like them, our vast expenditure of intellectual energy only leads us astray into the illusion that we humans really can control our destiny.

WEEK SEVEN

GATHERING DISCUSSION OUTLINE

A. Open session in prayer.

B. View video for this week's readings.

C. What general impressions and thoughts do you have after considering the video and reading the daily writings on these scriptures?

D. Discuss questions selected from the daily readings.

1. **KEY OBSERVATION:** The primary sin for which Babylon was judged was pride.

   DISCUSSION QUESTION: Why do you think pride has been designated as the deadliest of the seven deadly sins?

2. **KEY OBSERVATION:** Pride makes us think that we can do whatever we want and that we are not accountable for our actions.

   DISCUSSION QUESTION: What is it about pride that makes us think we can escape accountability?

3. **KEY OBSERVATION:** Many of life's tragedies are the result of uncontrolled desire.

   DISCUSSION QUESTION: How does the biblical understanding of life help us control our desires?

4. **KEY OBSERVATION:** It is very easy for us humans to live as though "I am, and there is no one besides me."

   DISCUSSION QUESTION: What are some of the manifestations and results of such an attitude? What is the Christian antidote to it?

5. **KEY OBSERVATION:** All human attempts to make ourselves secure will ultimately fail.

   DISCUSSION QUESTION: How does Christian faith address the problem of human insecurity?

E. What facts and information presented in the commentary portion of the lesson help you understand the weekly scripture?

F. Close session with prayer.

WEEK EIGHT

Isaiah 48

Israel Called to Listen to the Promises

INTRODUCTION

Just as Isaiah had shown what the implications of the case against the idols meant for Babylon (chap. 47), he now shows what they are for exiled Israel. What Yahweh's sole Godhood means is that the Israelites must not give up hope that they will be delivered. If they were to do that, succumbing to the heavy pressure to surrender their distinct identity and become absorbed into the imperial culture, then when the opportunity to go home actually came, they neither would, nor could accept it. Home? They were at home already. This clearly did happen to many because although there were a large number who did return, it is apparent that there were many who did not. But fortunately it did not happen to all the Judeans. Some of them did retain their distinctive identity and their (apparently) crazy hope. So when the hour came, they were ready.

A special feature of the chapter is repeated occurrences of words having to do with hearing (vv. 1, 6–8, 12, 14, 16, 18). There are ten occurrences in all. What is the reason for this? It is involved with a special feature of the Hebrew thought. In English we can make a distinction between sensing something and doing something about what we have sensed. Hebrew does not do that. For instance, in Hebrew thought if you remember something, you will act upon that memory. If you do not act, then whatever you may say, you have forgotten that thing. It is the same with hearing. If you truly hear a command, then you will obey it. If you don't obey, then whatever you say, you did not hear it. Thus, there are many places in English versions of the Old Testament where the word "obey" is used when the actual Hebrew is "listen." So here it is apparent that

God wants his people to take the appropriate action in the light of what he has demonstrated to be true in the previous chapters. He is the only God, and that means that he has the power to do what he has promised—namely, to deliver them out of the hands of the Babylonians. So what is the appropriate action to take, having heard this message? It is to keep themselves ready for the moment of deliverance. It is to refuse all the temptations to give up their distinctive identity and to maintain at all costs their sense of themselves as the unique people of God. For a narrative example of this, see Daniel 1–3.

ONE

Called by the Name of Israel

Isaiah 48:1–5 *Hear this, O house of Jacob, who are called by the name of Israel, and who came forth from the loins of Judah; who swear by the name of the* Lord, *and invoke the God of Israel, but not in truth or right.* ²*For they call themselves after the holy city, and lean on the God of Israel; the* Lord *of hosts is his name.*

³The former things I declared long ago, they went out from my mouth and I made them known; then suddenly I did them and they came to pass. ⁴Because I know that you are obstinate, and your neck is an iron sinew and your forehead brass, ⁵I declared them to you from long ago, before they came to pass I announced them to you, so that you would not say, "My idol did them, my carved image and my cast image commanded them."

Understanding the Word. In view of the generally gracious tone of God's address to his people in the previous chapters, the tone of this paragraph, and indeed of this entire chapter, seems rather harsh. What is going on? In the first place, this is a feature of the book that is relatively common. Isaiah will never allow a picture of a glorious future to allow his hearers to ignore the often harsh realities of the present. This is apparent in the first five chapters of the book, which are introductory. In 2:1–5 we are told that all the nations will come to Jerusalem to learn God's Torah (his instructions for life), and in 4:2–6 we are told that Jerusalem with be pure and holy, living under the canopy of God's protection. But before and after those future promises are pictures of the present, which depict Israel as hypocritical and proud, corrupt and thoroughly wicked. In short, the prophet is saying, we are never going to get to that glorious future unless somehow we allow God to come to grips with our present reality.

That same point is being made here. Yes, the promises of the future are secure. Cyrus will come, and he will permit all the captives to go home. But unless they face their present condition, and truly listen, they will be in no position to take advantage of the promises when they come. In fact, they might not even recognize them. What is the harsh reality that Isaiah is telling the exiles they will have to face? It is the fundamental fact of all Israelite history: they want the blessings of God without making any real surrender of themselves. They stood at Sinai and swore in blood that they would never break their covenant with God. Yet, within five weeks they were dancing around the image of a bull, praising it for having delivered them from Egypt. Why? Because they were afraid to trust a God they could not see. The covenant was broken and simple justice demanded that their blood oath be visited on them. But the God of grace did not do so. Yet that seems to have made little difference to the Hebrews; the rest of the Old Testament is the story of their repeatedly breaking their covenant until finally, after a thousand years, even the patience of God was exhausted. So these exiles must face the facts of their inheritance. They are called "Israel," the people of God. They love to take oaths (which they do not intend to keep) in the name of God. They call themselves "the people of Jerusalem, the holy city." But in fact, with them, as with their ancestors, there was a fundamental disconnect between the appearance and the reality, between the words and the facts. That had to be dealt with if they were going to be ready to give up the known and comfortable in Babylon and make a long and dangerous trip to a place most of them had never been.

At heart, the issue was unbelief. Here again is the feature of Hebrew I mentioned earlier. In English we can distinguish between intellectual belief and action based on belief. In Hebrew that is not possible, and neither is it in life. If we will not act in accordance with our beliefs, then in fact we do not believe what we say we believe. So the people could say that they believe in the transcendent God, who cannot be manipulated by human actions, while all the time they have idols in their tents (see Joshua 24:19–24). If something wonderful happens, they give their idol, the thing they have magically manipulated, the credit instead of giving it to God, who really did the thing (Isa. 48:5). This is why Yahweh predicts the future, he says, so that we cannot give the credit to what we have done for ourselves.

If the people are truly to believe, then they must address that disconnect between appearance and reality. They must live out the terms of their covenant. Their lives must reflect the character of God. It will not be enough merely to abstain from eating certain foods or refusing to work on Saturday, or swearing on the Bible. It will mean becoming truly dependent on Yahweh and being filled with a burning desire to be like him, to be his creatures in truth.

1. Paul speaks of having a form of religion, while denying the power thereof (see 2 Timothy 3:5). In the light of this passage, what does that mean? What is the power of the Christian religion?

2. When do we, saying we believe, in fact give evidence that we don't believe?

3. What are some examples of taking credit for ourselves instead of giving it to God?

T W O
You Hear New Things

Isaiah 48:6–8 *You have heard; now see all this; and will you not declare it? From this time forward I make you hear new things, hidden things that you have not known. ⁷They are created now, not long ago; before today you have never heard of them, so that you could not say, "I already knew them." ⁸You have never heard, you have never known, from of old your ear has not been opened. For I knew that you would deal very treacherously, and that from birth you were called a rebel.*

Understanding the Word. Once more Yahweh speaks of his ability to do things that have never happened before. The worldview of paganism simply has no room for that which is genuinely new. But perhaps someone says, "Surely the evolutionary view (which shares with ancient paganism the idea that this cosmos is all there is to reality) sees new things happening all the time." In fact, it does not. No "new" development is actually new; it is only a small mutation of that which had already existed. In this view what has always existed will always exist, perhaps going through an infinitude of changes, but in the end only a recombination of what has always been.

But Yahweh insists that he, the Creator, can bring into existence things that have never existed before. Now, perhaps you are becoming a little irritated at one more expression of this idea that Yahweh is not the cosmos. If so, that is certainly understandable, because it has been repeated in perhaps a dozen different ways in the previous eight chapters. But why is this the case? I believe it is because this is the absolutely fundamental issue in all reality. God is *not* this world. Start there and everything is different than if one begins at the only other possible starting point: this world is God (there being nothing else besides this world).

But the biblical view is very rare in the world. There are only three groups who take it: Christians, Jews, and Muslims. And all three of them got it from *one single source*: the book we call the Old Testament. Why should this view be so rare? Why are there not several sources for its origin? I believe it is because the idea is so difficult for us humans to accept. Above everything else it removes divine power from our control. If you and I are limited to this psycho-social-physical cosmos, and deity with all its power is not part of the cosmos, how do we control it? The frightening answer is that we cannot control it. Instead we must submit to it, trusting that it is acting in our best interests. For the children of Adam and Eve, that is nearly impossible to accept. We do not want to be dependent in any way. Notice the three terms that are used in verses 7 and 8: "knew," "treacherously," "rebel." All three of those are about independence and control. If something happens, we want to be able to say, "I already knew that." If God says, "I want you to commit yourself to me in a faithful covenant," we say, "I reserve the right to break all my promises whenever it suits me." If God says, "I have designed you to live in certain ways, and to be truly human, you must conform to them," we say with raised fist, "It's my life, and I will live it any way I choose."

Our ultimate rebellion, then, is to reimagine God. We will make the cosmos itself into God, imagining the transcendent one in our own image. We have done this for one reason: *so that we can control the sources of power* for ourselves. If deity is inherent in this world, then by manipulating the world, we can control divine power. This is why paganism, whether ancient or modern, is much the same around the world. It is the result of humans imagining reality in such a way as to bring it under control, the control of our minds ("I already knew that"), of our emotions ("I don't feel like keeping that promise"), and of our wills ("I don't care what you say; I *will* do what I want").

1. What are some of the ways we try to use our religious behavior to control God?

2. How was the coming of Jesus Christ the ultimate "new thing"?

3. What are some ways we try to make God in our own image, instead of allowing him to remake us in his image?

THREE

For My Name's Sake

Isaiah 48:9–13 *For my name's sake I defer my anger, for the sake of my praise I restrain it for you, so that I may not cut you off.* [10]*See, I have refined you, but not like silver; I have tested you in the furnace of adversity.* [11]*For my own sake, for my own sake, I do it, for why should my name be profaned? My glory I will not give to another.*

[12]*Listen to me, O Jacob, and Israel, whom I called: I am He; I am the first, and I am the last.* [13]*My hand laid the foundation of the earth, and my right hand spread out the heavens; when I summon them, they stand at attention.*

Understanding the Word. Given their long history of rebellion against Yahweh, how could the Judean exiles have any hope that he would deliver them? Should they not simply give up hope and stop resisting the lure of Babylonian culture? What could they possible do to wipe out that long history of breaking the covenant? Having been taken out of the holy land into unclean Babylon, they could not even offer the sacrifices that might magically change God's attitude toward them. To all of that God says that their deliverance does not depend on their somehow finding a way to make him forgive them. Just as he said in 43:25, so here he says again that he will forgive them for his own sake, for the sake of his name. As I said earlier, "name" in the ancient world did not first of all connote "label," as it does most commonly in English. Rather, it speaks of reputation, nature, and character. So what is Yahweh saying? He is saying that he does not forgive any of us because he has to or because we have done something to deserve it. He forgives us as an expression of his own nature. This is expressed powerfully in Hosea 11. In the first part of the chapter, Yahweh tells how he tenderly raised Israel from childhood and how they have repaid his care with rebellion, worshiping other gods. So he says that the end of his patience has come. The great nations that Israel has trusted will now be permitted to turn on Israel and destroy her. But then Yahweh cries out, in so many words, "How can I let you go?" (v. 8). If he were a human being whose love had been repeatedly rejected and abused, he might well be motivated by a desire for vengeance, a desire to see the offender wiped out. But that is it, he says. He is God, not man (v. 9). He is the Holy One, "the first and the last" (Isa. 48:12), the sole Creator, which means he is *not* like us, molded in our image. He is marked by an unfailing love, a love that is self-giving and self-denying. So, while punishment would come, it would not be that absolute destruction, that wiping off the face of the earth, that some raging human tyrant might demand to placate his outraged sense of power.

Thus when the apostle John said that God *is* love, he was not articulating some new, previously unheard-of idea. He was simply putting into propositional form the truth that had been emerging throughout Old Testament times. God forgives his people, including us, simply because he loves us. This is what John (and Jesus) call "perfect" or complete love (1 John 4:16–18; Matt. 5:43–48). Incomplete, or imperfect, love has to have someone else's love to get it started, and once started, it has to have someone else's love to keep going. But God's love is perfect, that is, complete in itself. It needs no one else's love to start, and it needs no one else's love to go on loving. This is his glory, the glory that none of this world's so-called gods can ever share.

1. What are some of the appropriate responses to an undeserved love like God's? First John 4:11 gives us one answer. Why is that appropriate, and what are some others?

2. Why is it so hard for us to accept a free forgiveness like this? Why do we keep on trying to earn it?

3. How does this passage address a statement like the following: In the Old Testament people were saved by keeping the law, but in the New Testament people are saved by grace. What was the function of the law, then?

FOUR
Who Has Declared These Things?

Isaiah 48:14–16 *Assemble, all of you, and hear! Who among them has declared these things? The* LORD *loves him; he shall perform his purpose on Babylon, and his arm shall be against the Chaldeans.* ¹⁵*I, even I, have spoken and called him, I have brought him, and he will prosper in his way.* ¹⁶*Draw near to me, hear this! From the beginning I have not spoken in secret, from the time it came to be I have been there. And now the Lord* GOD *has sent me and his spirit.*

Understanding the Word. Here is Yahweh's final statement about Cyrus, whom he has anointed (45:1) to be the deliverer of his people. Notice that his calling of Cyrus was an expression of his love. Yahweh loved Cyrus, in the sense that he lovingly chose this Persian to be the instrument of his love to the Judeans, and through them to the whole world. It will be interesting on the last day to see if Cyrus ever recognized that love and responded to it.

But the key point in this stanza is the repetition of words having to do with speaking (vv. 14–16). The point here is that God had clearly identified the deliverer far in advance. Scholars who deny the existence of predictive prophecy do so because of their conviction that it is an impossibility. There is no God outside of the cosmos; thus it is impossible for anyone to know the future, and even if it were possible, God does not speak. But of course those are *just* the points Isaiah is insisting upon. There *is* a God outside of the cosmos, who *does* know the future, and who *does* speak.

This latter idea cannot be made too much of. The gods do not speak except through oracles who chirp like birds and have to be interpreted, or through mediums who whisper ambiguities that could mean anything (Isa. 8:19; 29:4). The gods of earth cannot speak. Can the tree speak, or the sun, or the ocean? No, we must hear them in our own imagination. But that is not so of Yahweh. In fact, if he is to be known at all, he *must* speak. Since he is transcendent, he does not come to us in the intimations of nature. To be sure, when he has spoken, we can understand nature's speech correctly. This is the point of Psalm 19. But unless he finds a way to communicate with us, we can never know him and we will surely misread nature. But, praise his name, that is exactly what he has done. He has spoken! He spoke the worlds into existence; he spoke with Adam and Eve, our parents in life; he spoke to Abraham and Sarah, our parents in faith; he spoke to David the forerunner; he spoke to the prophets, and so on down through time, until he has finally, and triumphantly, spoken to us in Christ. The apostle John was not merely playing with words when he chose to call Jesus "the Word" (John 1:1). Jesus the Christ is the ultimate speech of Yahweh to his creation.

So the specific prediction of Cyrus, even to giving his name, is the evidence that there is a God outside of time who knows the future and who has communicated his will and his nature to us. Isaiah puts himself forward as the evidence of this when he says, "[Yahweh] GOD has sent me and his Spirit" (Isa. 48:16). This prophet does not chirp and mutter, speaking in mysteries and secrets that require special skills to understand, but empowered by the Spirit of God, he speaks the simple and transparent truth. Everything vital to our life and salvation has been encapsulated in the written Word of God. We can know why we are here, what life is about, and how life is meant to be lived. Poet William Wordsworth said, "The world is too much with us," and it is, but we have the message that God has spoken to all of his creatures, and that means that like the Judean exiles, we ought to be shaped by it, and not by the culture around us.

1. What are some practical ways that we can be "in" the world, but not "of" it, as Jesus said (John 17:14–15)?

2. Across the years God's people have known the experience of being spoken to by God. Have you experienced that? What was it like? How can we be sure it is God?

3. What can nature tell us about God once we know him through the Word?

FIVE

Go out from Babylon

Isaiah 48:17–22 *Thus says the LORD, your Redeemer, the Holy One of Israel: I am the LORD your God, who teaches you for your own good, who leads you in the way you should go. ¹⁸O that you had paid attention to my commandments! Then* *your prosperity would have been like a river, and your success like the waves of the sea;* ¹⁹*your offspring would have been like the sand, and your descendants like its grains; their name would never be cut off or destroyed from before me.*

²⁰*Go out from Babylon, flee from Chaldea, declare this with a shout of joy, proclaim it, send it forth to the end of the earth; say, "The* L<small>ORD</small> *has redeemed his servant Jacob!"* ²¹*They did not thirst when he led them through the deserts; he made water flow for them from the rock; he split open the rock and the water gushed out.*

²²*"There is no peace," says the* L<small>ORD</small>*, "for the wicked."*

Understanding the Word. In this, the final word of this section, chapters 41–48, the prophet takes a very comprehensive view to emphasize the importance of listening. In the first place, he says, none of this—the destruction of Jerusalem and the exile in Babylon—need ever have happened. If they had "paid attention"—listened—long ago, then all of the promises to Abraham and his descendants would have been theirs without interruption. They would not have seen their children slaughtered before their eyes, nor now to be forced to wonder whether the line of Abraham was going to disappear in Babylon.

However, that having happened, if they would listen now, then the God of grace would do the impossible once again. Just as he had brought water out of rocks for their ancestors in the Sinai wilderness, so he would take these people out of the hand of Babylon. In spite of the sin that had brought them to this sad place, Yahweh would do what is right, given his own nature, and would redeem them. In any case, let them not *repeat* the failure of that first generation in the wilderness and refuse to listen this time. Even though the ancient Israelites had failed that first test, God still intends to redeem these their descendants, and bless them. But they must not surrender their faith in him now.

One of the frequent features of the book of Isaiah is the piling up of names and titles for God. Clearly, the prophet wants to convey to us, his hearers, the rich character of Yahweh. Here, he does this in the opening line of the stanza: "[Yahweh], your Redeemer, the Holy One of Israel" (v. 17). Like the stanza as a whole, there is a very comprehensive tone here. Who is this God? He is utterly transcendent: he is the I AM, upon whose existence the existence of every other thing depends; he is the Holy One, who is completely other than every other thing in the universe. But he is also immediately present: he is *your* Redeemer, the Holy One *of Israel*. This is what the Greek philosophers could not comprehend. How could the transcendent one bind himself to an insignificant, rebellious little people group and yet retain his transcendence. Impossible? Yes, but, praise be to God, true! For here is the source of hope that has breathed through this entire section. If Yahweh is but one of the gods, one of the forces of the cosmos wearing a humanlike mask, there is no possibility of our ever being released from all the other cosmic forces that hold us captive. But if he is Yahweh, the God from beyond the cosmos, who holds all things in his hands, *and* if his name is love, then there is *always* hope, even, best of all, eternal hope.

1. How do we put together the Old Testament promises of blessing for obedience with Jesus' statement that in this world his followers "will have trouble" (John 16:33 NIV)?

2. What does redemption mean for you in the light of the Bible's teachings?

3. What are some of the things God has redeemed you from?

COMMENTARY NOTES

As I mentioned earlier, one of Isaiah's favorite devices is the "piling up" of names and titles for God. One of those titles is Yahweh of Hosts ("the LORD of hosts," 48:2). It is very frequent in the book, occurring some fifty times. It is also common in Jeremiah and in Haggai, Zechariah, and Malachi. Oddly, it does not occur at all in Ezekiel or Daniel. Since most modern readers do not have a good idea what a "host" is (apart from someone who welcomes guests, which it is not here!), the NIV has translated it as "LORD Almighty" which is not incorrect, as we will see, but loses some of the impact and color that the Hebrew carries.

In the Old Testament, a "host" is a multitude. We sometimes use it that way when we say "there were a host of people at the game." In particular, the Bible uses the term in two ways: for an army and for the stars. In the latter case, the text is saying that Yahweh is over all the host of stars. The significance of this is that the pagans thought that the stars were gods. But the Bible, as in Isaiah 40:26, says that God has named them and calls them to order. They all appear when he calls the roll. He alone is God, and the whole host of heaven does his bidding. Here is where the two concepts of stars and armies come together. All the armies of heaven are at Yahweh's command. One example of this is found in 2 Kings 6:15–19, where the armies of heaven have surrounded the Syrian army that was trying to take Elisha captive. This is also the idea behind

Jesus' statement to Peter that if he wanted to escape the cross, he would not need Peter's sword but could call on twelve legions of angels to come and deliver him (Matt. 26:52–53).

So this is the meaning of "Yahweh of Hosts." All the limitless forces of the universe are his to command at any moment. So the NIV's "LORD Almighty" does express the idea. But the NLT's "the LORD of Heaven's Armies" preserves the force of the image in a better way.

Looking at another verse now, the mention of "the former things I declared long ago" (v. 3) alongside "before today you have never heard of them" (v. 7) seems contradictory. Those who believe that chapters 40–66 were written during the exile hold that "the former things" were what Isaiah had said during his lifetime (circa 700 BC), while "today" refers to things that the anonymous prophet conventionally known as "Second Isaiah" was saying circa 545 BC.

While this is certainly a possibility, it is not the only one. Another possibility is that "the former things" were prophetic promises given in the distant past, such as, for instance, the promise given to Abraham that he would have many descendants and that they would possess the land of Canaan. "Today" would refer to Isaiah's time when he was predicting the completely new idea that not only would the Israelites go into captivity, but, something completely unheard of, they would also be restored from that captivity. Since the people of Isaiah's day denied that they would go into captivity, the prediction of a return would have had no meaning for them at all. But when the day came that they were in captivity, those words would come to them with a new immediacy.

Now look at the sentence "There is no peace . . . for the wicked" (v. 22); it is also found in 57:21. Very early in the interpretation of Isaiah, it was observed that the two occurrences serve to divide chapters 40–66 into three nine-chapter segments: 40–48; 49–57; 58–66. Some commentaries, especially older ones, follow that structure in their comments. However, the content of the material does not really conform to that division. That content more naturally falls into two divisions (as we are taking it in these studies): 40–55, and 56–66.

The sentence fits the context of chapter 57 very well. Verse 19 says that God extends peace to the far and the near. But then verses 20 and 21 are at pains to say that such a promise does not extend to the wicked, for whom there is no peace.

On the other hand, the sentence does not fit into the end of chapter 48 at all. Here, the final stanza is calling on the exiles to leave Babylon with the confidence that just as God had provided for their ancestors when they went out of Egypt, so he would provide for them. Perhaps if there had been some statement about the judgment that came on the first generation in the wilderness because of unbelief, that would have provided some context for the statement of no peace for the wicked. But there is no such statement, or even the hint of one.

It seems to me that what happened was this: at some early point (48:21 is already in the Dead Sea scroll of Isaiah), an editor or copyist noticed that what is now 57:21 occurred at a point where two-thirds of what is now chapters 40–66 preceded it and one-third of the material followed it (verse numbers and chapter divisions only come in the first millennium after Christ). So it occurred to him to insert the sentence where it would divide that previous material in half and thus produce equal thirds.

WEEK EIGHT

GATHERING DISCUSSION OUTLINE

A. Open session in prayer.

B. View video for this week's readings.

C. What general impressions and thoughts do you have after considering the video and reading the daily writings on these scriptures?

D. Discuss questions selected from the daily readings.

1. **KEY OBSERVATION:** One of the great dangers in the life of a believer is to act as though something were true in our walk with God when it is not.

   DISCUSSION QUESTION: Paul speaks of having a form of religion, while denying the "power" thereof (see 2 Timothy 3:5). In the light of this passage, what does that mean? What is the power of the Christian religion?

2. **KEY OBSERVATION:** Since he is uniquely transcendent, God cannot be controlled by our behavior. But this is very difficult for us to accept.

   DISCUSSION QUESTION: What are some of the ways we try to use our religious behavior to control God?

3. **KEY OBSERVATION:** God forgives us for his own sake, not because of anything we have done to deserve it.

DISCUSSION QUESTION: What are some of the appropriate responses to love like that? First John 4:11 gives us one answer. Why is that appropriate, and what are some others?

4. **KEY OBSERVATION:** We should live in the confidence that all God has spoken is certain. That means we should not become acculturated to this world.

   DISCUSSION QUESTION: What are some practical ways in which we can be "in" the world, but not "of" it, as Jesus said (John 17:14–15)?

5. **KEY OBSERVATION:** If we follow God's leading and obey his commands, we will enjoy a life of blessing.

   DISCUSSION QUESTION: How do we put together the Old Testament promises of blessing for obedience with Jesus' statement that in this world his followers "will have trouble" (John 16:33 NIV)?

E. What facts and information presented in the commentary portion of the lesson help you understand the weekly scripture?

F. Close session with prayer.

WEEK NINE

Isaiah 49:1–9, 13–19, 23–26; 50:1–3

Israel Not Forgotten

INTRODUCTION

In chapters 41–48 Yahweh had established his desire, his ability, and his intention to deliver Israel from its captivity in Babylon and, by the power of Cyrus, his anointed one, to restore their city and temple. Furthermore, he had reiterated at length that he had not cast Israel off, but that they were his chosen servants to, among other things, bear witness that he alone is God, and that there is no other.

However, those promises raise another question: What about Israel's sin? Israel is in captivity because of its sin. How can unholy Israel be the servants of holy Yahweh? But perhaps someone says, "Well, they have been punished, so they have 'paid' for their sin." But have they? Perhaps one can pay one's "debt to society" with some sort of punishment, but how does one restore a relationship with those against whom one has sinned? But beyond that, when one's sin is against God, can mere punishment ever redress the balances of divine justice? And there is one more issue: unless there is some change in Israel's condition, taking them home will simply mean another repetition of the previous one thousand years.

Chapters 49–55 speak to these questions. They answer by saying that the means whereby unholy Israel can become holy servants is the ideal Servant, the ideal Israel, who will be for Israel what actual Israel could never be on its own. We were first introduced to this Servant in 42:1–9, where I suggested that we were being given a preview of the answer to the question as it was already raised in chapter 41. Now, in chapters 49–55, we are given a full explanation of how the Servant will restore the relationship between Israel and

Yahweh; indeed, between humanity and Yahweh. This explanation is centered around three poems about the Servant. They are found in 49:1–12; 50:4–9; and 52:13–53:12.

Although deliverance language continues to be used in this section, it is no longer deliverance from Babylon that is in view, but deliverance back into a relationship with Yahweh. In 49:1–52:12 there is increasing anticipation that deliverance is going to be made available; then in 54–55 there is glad invitation to participate in the deliverance. When we ask what accounts for the change from anticipation to invitation, we need only look to the intervening section, 52:13–53:12, where the work of the Servant is finally and fully explained.

Isaiah 49:1–13 bears a remarkable similarity to 42:1–13. It is somewhat like the musical device called a reprise. It picks up an earlier melody and then carries it forward. Here it is as though the prophet is saying, "Remember when I introduced this theme back in chapter 42? Let's pick that idea up again and see where it will lead us." In the first and second studies that follow, we will look at that reprise as it sets the stage for moving forward. Then the third through the fifth studies will explore how that way forward begins to be treated in the rest of the section.

ONE

Named in My Mother's Womb

Isaiah 49:1–5 *Listen to me, O coastlands, pay attention, you peoples from far away! The LORD called me before I was born, while I was in my mother's womb he named me. ²He made my mouth like a sharp sword, in the shadow of his hand he hid me; he made me a polished arrow, in his quiver he hid me away. ³And he said to me, "You are my servant, Israel, in whom I will be glorified." ⁴But I said, "I have labored in vain, I have spent my strength for nothing and vanity; yet surely my cause is with the LORD, and my reward with my God."*

⁵And now the LORD says, who formed me in the womb to be his servant, to bring Jacob back to him, and that Israel might be gathered to him, for I am honored in the sight of the LORD, and my God has become my strength . . .

Understanding the Word. In 42:6, the point was made that this ideal Servant has been specifically called. Here that point is reiterated, but made more vivid:

the Servant was called "in my mother's womb," and his character ("name") and the nature of his ministry were defined there before birth. If we believe, as Christians have for two thousand years, that this Servant is Jesus, it is very easy to see what Matthew was thinking of when he recorded the words of the angel to Joseph before Jesus' birth, "You are to name him Jesus, for he will save his people from their sins" (Matt. 1:21). In chapter 42 the quiet, and unassuming, yet determined manner in which the Servant would carry out his work was discussed. Here it is apparent that even though empowered by God himself (49:2–3), the work would seem to be ineffective (v. 4a). This is where the clear sense of calling coupled with total commitment would be so important to the Servant: his "cause" and his "reward" were with Yahweh (v. 4b; see also 5b) so he could trustfully leave the outcome of his work in God's hands. And what would that work be? Here the possibility that we discussed in regard to 42:6 ("a covenant to the people") is made fully explicit. The Servant's work, as directed by Yahweh, is to bring Jacob/Israel back to Yahweh (49:5). If there were any question as to whether this is simply an alternate description of the nation (the negative descriptions giving a "before" picture, and the four positive ones an "after" picture), this verse coupled with verses 6 and 8 (see the commentary that follows) and 42:6 settles that question decisively. Israel cannot bring Israel back to God, and Israel cannot be a covenant with Israel.

But if that is so, why is this Servant called "Israel" in verse 3? Some commentators, accepting the logic of the point I have just made, suggest that it must be a textual error, while others, glossing over the logic just presented, insist that since the name occurs, the description here (vv. 1–9) *must* be of the nation, regardless of the problems. The first alternative is not supported by the textual evidence, and the second is flat self-contradictory. So what *is* being said? It is being said that this Servant is the True Israel. He will be for Israel and the world what Israel was never able to be in itself. He will serve Yahweh in true joyful submission as Israel never could. He will display Yahweh to the world as Israel was never able to do.

1. How does a sense of doing God's will empower us to survive difficult situations?

2. How would you relate the Servant's being "called from the womb" to the doctrine of the virgin birth?

3. How does Yahweh's statement that he will forgive us for his own sake (43:25; 48:9) relate to the work of the Servant in restoring God's people to himself?

TWO

You Hear New Things

Isaiah 49:6–9, 13 *[H]e says, "It is too light a thing that you should be my servant to raise up the tribes of Jacob and to restore the survivors of Israel; I will give you as a light to the nations, that my salvation may reach to the end of the earth."*

[7] Thus says the LORD, the Redeemer of Israel and his Holy One, to one deeply despised, abhorred by the nations, the slave of rulers, "Kings shall see and stand up, princes, and they shall prostrate themselves, because of the LORD, who is faithful, the Holy One of Israel, who has chosen you."

[8] Thus says the LORD: In a time of favor I have answered you, on a day of salvation I have helped you; I have kept you and given you as a covenant to the people, to establish the land, to apportion the desolate heritages; [9] saying to the prisoners, "Come out," to those who are in darkness, "Show yourselves." They shall feed along the ways, on all the bare heights shall be their pasture . . .

[13] Sing for joy, O heavens, and exult, O earth; break forth, O mountains, into singing! For the LORD has comforted his people, and will have compassion on his suffering ones.

Understanding the Word. In this portion of the second Servant poem, the Servant further recounts what Yahweh has said to him in commissioning him. He had already said some of that indirectly in verse 5, but now he reports it in the form of a direct quotation. In fact, the Servant's ministry will not be limited to the nation of Israel. That restoration is not a big enough job! No, the Servant will be "a light to the nations" so that Yahweh's "salvation may reach to the end of the earth" (v. 6). Again, this is not the nation of Israel, but neither is it any other merely human individual. The statement is in close accord with 42:1, where it was said the Servant would bring "justice" to the nations. Whoever this Servant is, his ministry has worldwide implications. As I said earlier, we are no longer talking about deliverance of some thousands of Judean exiles from bondage in Babylon. Now we are talking about a deliverance from something that afflicts the entire earth, as represented by Israel. That affliction is the alienation from God on account of sin. Israel cannot deliver itself from that, let alone deliver the whole earth.

But what about verse 7; could these statements not be applied to the nation? Yes, they could, especially in the light of some of the promises found in chapter 60 (see especially 60:14). However, the context here (as well as the similar statements in 52:14–15, which are undoubtedly speaking of the Servant) argues against that conclusion. Note also that the combination of titles, which is almost identical to that addressed to the nation in 48:17, is spoken of "him" here, not "you" as is more common in addressing the nation. What is being said is a further incremental revelation of the contradictory experience of the Servant. On the one hand, he will be "despised" and "rejected" (53:1–3). But on the other, kings will worship him (52:15). We ask how this could be, and the prophet answers that it is because Yahweh, the Holy One of Israel, can be relied on to care for the Servant whom he has called (vv. 7–8). We are moved here to think of the apostle Paul's famous hymn in Philippians 2:6–11, where he pictures Christ going from the heights to the depths and back again.

As the Servant's ministry is described in verses 8–9, our minds are led forward to Isaiah's final words about the Messiah in 61:1–3, where the Messiah's ministry is to set the captives free and bid those who dwell in darkness to come out. The lyric continues on through verses 10–12, but the sense is the same as that found in verse 9: the Servant is pictured as the Good Shepherd (see 40:11; John 10:1–15) who leads his sheep along easy pathways, protecting them from every danger, with some coming to him from the ends of the earth (Isa. 49:12).

Finally, just as in chapter 42, this revelation of the Servant is followed by an ecstatic hymn of praise (v. 13). As there (42:10–13), the whole cosmos joins in the celebration, for just as the creation has been affected by the fall of humanity, so the creation will be affected by our redemption. We are not speaking here merely of exiles returning to their land. We are speaking of all creation having received the comfort (encouragement, see 40:1) and compassion of the Creator, who has made it possible through the work of the Servant for his estranged children to come home to his arms.

1. How is Christ's work in making forgiveness available an encouragement ("comfort") to you?

2. Do you agree that this passage (along with vv. 1–5) is not talking about the nation of Israel? Why or why not?

3. I have suggested some ways in which verses 1–12 accords with the ministry of Christ. Can you think of others?

THREE

Inscribed on the Palms of My Hands

Isaiah 49:14–19 *But Zion said, "The LORD has forsaken me, my Lord has forgotten me."* [15]*Can a woman forget her nursing child, or show no compassion for the child of her womb? Even these may forget, yet I will not forget you.* [16]*See, I have inscribed you on the palms of my hands; your walls are continually before me.* [17]*Your builders outdo your destroyers, and those who laid you waste go away from you.* [18]*Lift up your eyes all around and see; they all gather, they come to you. As I live, says the LORD, you shall put all of them on like an ornament, and like a bride you shall bind them on.*

[19]*Surely your waste and your desolate places and your devastated land— surely now you will be too crowded for your inhabitants, and those who swallowed you up will be far away.*

Understanding the Word. Exiled Israel's response to the lyrical promises contained in verses 9–13 is reminiscent of the responses in the book of Malachi. There, whenever Yahweh makes some great affirmative statement, such as the "O, how I have loved you!" of Malachi 1:2 (author's translation), the response is one of cynicism and doubt. In that case, it is "How have you loved us?" It is not a request for information. It is more of an "Oh, yeah? Well, we don't see any evidence of it!" So here, the response is, "Get down off your lyrical high horse, Isaiah. God hasn't redeemed us, either from Babylon or from our sin. We are just the same people we were yesterday, in the same mess we were in yesterday. The fact is, God doesn't even know who we are." This is the unbelief that we talked about in the previous lesson, on chapter 48. This would be the attitude that, if maintained, would cause them to give up their distinctive faith and practices and would leave them to simply subside into the Babylonian mass.

But it is certainly easy to understand why they would feel that way, isn't it? We don't see any of these wonderful promises "on the ground," where we are. Life is still the same humdrum round from one day to the next. The result is often a downward spiral; because we won't live in faith, God can't do the things that would encourage more faith. That was the case with Jesus in Nazareth. The people wanted to see miracles so they could believe that this really was the hometown boy made good. But in their collective heart of hearts, they really did not believe he was any more than just another hometown boy. As a result, Jesus could not do the miracles they demanded (Luke 4:22–30).

In response to that cynicism, Yahweh responds that he could no more forget his people than a nursing mother could forget her child, and even if she did, he would not. His attachment to them is more than that of a mother to her child. It is one of complete, undeserved, unfailing love. So he says that their names are written on his palms. This is the opposite of the master's name being tattooed on the slave's hand. Here, as we saw earlier, the Master, the Lord, chooses to be identified by the names of his slaves. He is the Holy One *of Israel.*

The metaphor then shifts as Yahweh speaks of his people in terms of the city of salvation (see Isa. 26:1–2; 60:18). The devastated city, devoid of inhabitants, will be restored, and the descendants that the cynics said were gone forever will come flooding back, unimpeded by any of those former enemies, all of them now gone.

Has God forgotten his people on account of their sin? Will he perhaps take them home physically, but allow them to remain estranged from them? Never! They are precious to him, and he will do whatever it takes through his Servant to bring them to his heart, and to fill the city of salvation with his own faithful children.

1. Why does genuine belief have to precede divine action on our behalf? What is the human problem that requires this sequence?

2. Why is it easier to think that Yahweh has forgotten us than to believe that he loves us?

3. What is the difference between belief seeking confirmation, and doubt demanding proof?

FOUR

You Will Know That I Am Yahweh

Isaiah 49:23–26 *Kings shall be your foster fathers, and their queens your nursing mothers. With their faces to the ground they shall bow down to you, and lick the dust of your feet. Then you will know that I am the* Lord; *those who wait for me shall not be put to shame.*

24Can the prey be taken from the mighty, or the captives of a tyrant be rescued? 25But thus says the Lord: *Even the captives of the mighty shall be taken, and the prey of the tyrant be rescued; for I will contend with those who contend with you, and I will save your children. 26I will make your oppressors eat their own flesh, and they shall be drunk with their own blood as with wine. Then all flesh shall know that I am the* Lord *your Savior, and your Redeemer, the Mighty One of Jacob.*

Understanding the Word. In these verses, Isaiah continues the theme that he began to discuss in verses 12 and 19; namely, that the promises to Abraham of a great progeny would not fail, but that God would bring them into his city from every corner of the earth. But the objection might be raised, "We are such a small people, and our enemies are so great." This was true physically, but perhaps even more so spiritually. As the apostle Paul tells us, we are opposed by "principalities and powers in high places" (Eph. 6:12, paraphrased). Even though the Bible, wisely, chooses not to make a lot of this, we still need to know that there are evil spiritual forces around us seeking to destroy us.

So how are these promises of a great host of children of Abraham (see John 8:39; Galatians 3:7) possible? The answer to that question is the unanswerable power of Yahweh. That power will be displayed in a way that is unmistakable. Twice here we see the phrase "know that I am [Yahweh]" (vv. 23, 26). First it is that "you" will know, and then it is that "all flesh" will know. Know what? Know that I am Yahweh. This is different from the connotation of our English translation, "Lord." That suggests we will know he is sovereign, that he is King, Master, Controller, and so forth. He is all of those, but knowing that he is *Yahweh* is so much more. He is *all things*: life, hope, truth, joy, memory, creativity, peace, receptivity, dynamic power, perfect love, and on and on. He is *I AM*! Yahweh says we will know who he is when he

128

defeats all the powers of evil in the cosmos. Who could do that except the one who is the very source and end of the cosmos?

This is what Jesus Christ, the Servant, has done. Again, it is the apostle Paul who so vividly paints this picture: "He disarmed the rulers and authorities and made a public example of them, triumphing over them in it" (Col. 2:15). The picture is of a victorious Roman general who is riding in his chariot in a "triumph," a victory parade, with his defeated, helpless enemies marching to their death in chains behind him. God says to the exiles and to all of us that if we will "wait" trustfully, he will break the power of evil in the world at large, but also in our own lives and restore us to himself. In so doing, will make a way for "all flesh" to participate in that same victory. In 48:17, speaking to Israel, he called himself "your Redeemer." Now he says "all flesh" (49:26) will recognize that fact and, as we will see momentarily, will be enabled to participate in it for themselves.

As I noted earlier, the language of deliverance continues to be used throughout this section even though Babylon itself does not appear in these chapters. I have been emphasizing spiritual deliverance because I think that is the central thrust. However, I do not want to gloss over the fact that the physical deliverance was still an essential part of what the prophet was talking about. God is not going to deliver them from their sins and leave them in Babylon, any more than he is going to deliver them from Babylon and leave them in their sins. So, just as the principalities and powers that hold us in spiritual bondage have been defeated, so the powers that would have held Israel in physical bondage were defeated as well. God is the God of the whole world, and his deliverance is intended to be real in every sphere.

1. Where are some areas of your life that you feel tempted to believe that God's power cannot reach? How will you go about applying his promises to those areas?

2. What personal experiences have caused you to know that he is Yahweh?

3. What prevents us from experiencing Yahweh's delivering power in our lives? What steps do we need to take to address that?

FIVE

Is My Hand Shortened?

Isaiah 50:1–3 *Thus says the* Lord: *Where is your mother's bill of divorce with which I put her away? Or which of my creditors is it to whom I have sold you? No, because of your sins you were sold, and for your transgressions your mother was put away.* ²*Why was no one there when I came? Why did no one answer when I called? Is my hand shortened, that it cannot redeem? Or have I no power to deliver? By my rebuke I dry up the sea, I make the rivers a desert; their fish stink for lack of water, and die of thirst.* ³*I clothe the heavens with blackness, and make sackcloth their covering.*

Understanding the Word. With this, the final stanza in this unit, the prophet circles back to the underlying question of the first verse in the unit. That underlying question was, "Given all these great promises, why are we still in captivity to our sins?" Their conclusion there was: "Well, Yahweh has forgotten us." That response was disposed of both immediately and at length. So now a second, two-pronged alternative is proposed. This one also impugns Yahweh, suggesting that he had arbitrarily divorced the mother and sold the children, and therefore had no real interest in getting them back.

Yahweh responds to these charges by saying there was nothing arbitrary about what he had done. If they will produce the divorce certificate, they will see the list of the mother's "transgressions" there. Furthermore, if there were a bill of sale, it would show that the people had been sold to satisfy the debt of their own "sins." So if they are still in bondage, it is not because of Yahweh's arbitrary attitude toward them.

Where does the true cause of their condition lie? It lies with them, according to verses 2 and 3. On the one hand, when Yahweh has come to them, they have not responded with repentance and faith. They have not dared to believe that he really wanted to save them, or that he could. So when he has called to them, they have remained in lethargy. There is a pattern here: God's call, our faith, his action.

Perhaps their failure to listen (see chapter 48) and believe is because of their deep doubt that he is able to do anything about their sinful condition. We see here a metaphor that will be very important in the subsequent chapters.

This is the metaphor of the "hand" (used interchangeably with "arm"; see the following commentary on 51:5). The Hebrew term *yad*, translated "hand" in English, has a slightly different denotation than English "hand," in that it can denote everything from the elbow to the fingertips. So, for instance, the one who "acts high-*hand*edly" in Numbers 15:30 refers to one who acts with a raised fist. Here, then, for Yahweh's "hand" to be "shortened" would mean that he would not have the strength to accomplish his will. But in fact, he does have all strength, so much so that he can do the impossible: he can make seas and rivers dry, and he can make the brilliant heavens dark. Once again he is emphasizing that his power is in no way constrained by the manner in which mere cosmic powers have always operated. The Creator, standing outside the cosmos, can do new things.

1. Think of some examples in which we today blame God for our condition or situation. How do we go about changing those attitudes?

2. Do you have some issues that you think God is unable to address? Why do you feel that way? What needs to change?

3. Can you think of situations in your own life or in the lives of others in which God's power to deliver has been displayed?

COMMENTARY NOTES

Some people say that one of the distinctions between Isaiah chapters 1–39 and 40–55 is the distinction between the royal Messiah figure in the former section and the Servant figure in the latter. However, comparison of the two reveals that the distinctions are not so clear as some maintain, and that there are more similarities than some recognize.

Above all, we should note the non-regal character of the Messiah in the earlier chapters. In fact, the author seems to be at pains to distance this King from other kings. This is seen first of all in the picture in chapter 9. We are told that the two kings of Israel and Syria are attacking Judah and that King Ahaz of Judah has made a deal with the real threat, the emperor of Assyria. But Isaiah says that Ahaz should trust God, who will send a *child*-king, and that young king will put a stop to all warfare. A child to confront a military colossus?

This thought is carried further in chapter 11. The mighty forest, Assyria, had been cut down at the end of chapter 10, to be replaced by what or whom? It is "whom," as the following chapter makes clear. But who is this replacement? He is someone who does not act like any ordinary king. He is only a "shoot" or a "branch," not some mighty tree (v. 1). His actions are not shaped by a desire for power and splendor but by the fear of the Lord (vv. 2 and 3). He has a Spirit-enabled power of perception that probes far beneath appearances (vv. 2 and 3). As

for the "rod" with which he subdues the enemy (v. 4)? It is his mouth, his capacity to speak. His power is not coercion, but persuasion.

In chapter 32, we see a similar theme. In the context of justice and righteousness, the court of the King will be marked by unusual perception and judgment. There will be a transparent nobility that will be in sharp contrast to the typical court, where petty intrigues and treachery are often the norm.

When these features are compared with those used to describe the Servant in the so-called Servant Songs (42:1–9; 49:1–12; 50:4–9; 52:13–53:12), there is a marked similarity. To be sure, the element of suffering does not appear in the passages discussed earlier. But the general attitude of humility, yet capacity, the reliance on God and his Spirit, the importance of perception and sensitivity, the significance of speech (note especially the mouth as sword, 49:2; see 11:4) all suggest not two contrasting figures, but rather two complementary ones: the King who serves, and the Servant who rules (see Mark 10:44; John 13:13–14).

Next, let's look at the phrase "then you/they will know I am Yahweh"; it is an extremely important one in the Old Testament because it underlines the mode of revelation in the book. What do I mean by that? Elsewhere, I have argued that the only satisfactory explanation for the unique doctrine of a transcendent, yet personal God that is found in the Old

Testament is the one it itself gives: divine revelation. The Hebrews tell us that God entered into the human-historical experience in both act and word and showed them who he is and what life is about. In other words, God showed them these truths in the context of their experience. This is the importance of the word "know" here, because in Hebrew this word speaks almost exclusively of learning something through experience.

The first place we encounter the phrase is in the book of Exodus. There it occurs in one form or another about a dozen times between chapters 6 and 18. The point is that God was going to give knowledge, both to the Israelites and the Egyptians, through historical acts explained in speech. What they were going to learn by experience is that he alone is the source and the goal of all being (I AM) and that everything the Egyptians worshiped was, in fact, only cosmic forces under the direct control of Yahweh.

The other place where we encounter concentrations of the phrase is in the book of Ezekiel. It occurs there more than fifty times! Ezekiel is rather clearly expressing the idea that Israel has not learned this truth, and to learn it, they will have to have to go through another captivity like the one in Egypt and another deliverance like the one from Egypt. So he says that when they have experienced Yahweh's judgment in history, they will know he is Yahweh, and likewise, when they have experienced his deliverance in history they will know that he is Yahweh. Isaiah is clearly making the second part of this point in our passage here (49:19, 26). The experience of deliverance, against all the odds, will be concrete proof that Yahweh alone is God.

The thing I want to emphasize here is the importance of history to the validity of revelation. What are the Hebrews saying to us? They are saying that the reason they know their God is I AM is because of what he has done in their history. But suppose, as all too many scholars say today, that virtually all of Israel's so-called history before the time of King Hezekiah (700 BC, including the exodus and a good bit of it after that time) is pure fiction. What then? Where did the idea of a personal, transcendent God, who is the source and goal of all being, come from? And if it did not come out of real historical experience, where did the Israelites, alone among the people of the ancient world, get the idea of couching their religious sentiments in the garb of historical fiction? Isn't it simpler to believe the Bible's own account of itself: *You know that I am Yahweh because you have experienced me in your own history?*

WEEK NINE

GATHERING DISCUSSION OUTLINE

A. Open session in prayer.

B. View video for this week's readings.

C. What general impressions and thoughts do you have after considering the video and reading the daily writings on these scriptures?

D. Discuss questions selected from the daily readings.

   1. **KEY OBSERVATION:** The Servant's confidence in his calling enabled him to accept the apparent failure of his mission.

   DISCUSSION QUESTION: How does a sense of doing God's will empower us to survive difficult situations?

   2. **KEY OBSERVATION:** The work of the Servant brings comfort (encouragement) to all the world.

   DISCUSSION QUESTION: How is Christ's work in making forgiveness available an encouragement ("comfort") to you?

   3. **KEY OBSERVATION:** God's capacity to act in our particular situations is conditioned upon our response in faith to him.

   DISCUSSION QUESTION: Why does genuine belief have to precede divine action on our behalf? What is the human problem that requires this sequence?

4. **KEY OBSERVATION:** God in Christ has defeated every enemy that would hold us in bondage.

   DISCUSSION QUESTION: What prevents us from experiencing Yahweh's delivering power in our lives? What steps do we need to take to address that?

   5. **KEY OBSERVATION:** It is very easy for us to blame God if we are not experiencing deliverance in some area of our lives.

      DISCUSSION QUESTION: Think of some examples in which we blame God today for our condition or situation. How do we go about changing those attitudes?

E. What facts and information presented in the commentary portion of the lesson help you understand the weekly scripture?

F. Close session with prayer.

WEEK TEN

Isaiah 50:4–11; 51:1–5, 13–17, 22; 52:1–12

Put on Your Beautiful Garments, O Jerusalem

INTRODUCTION

Just as 49:1–50:3 were composed of the second Servant song and reflections upon it and its implications, so 50:4–52:12 are composed of the third song (50:4–9) and reflections upon it and its implications. In this case, however, the reflections are at greater length. We should also recognize that there is a cumulating effect from 49:1 straight through to 52:12. Yahweh's insistence that he will restore his people to himself, defeating their sin, rises in intensity, and with it there is an increasing sense of anticipation among the people. Both of these reach their climax in 52:1–12.

The third Servant song reveals something more of the physical and emotional suffering that the Servant would undergo in fulfilling his mission. This was hinted at in the first and second, and comes to its completion in the fourth (52:13–53:12). This third song, emphasizing the Servant's determined obedience at all costs, provides the basis for Yahweh's appeal in the following verses. That appeal is especially addressed to those who are seeking to do right (50:10; 51:1, 4, 7), but who at the same time are laboring under a deep sense of guilt and failure (51:17). God assures them that his righteousness is going to be revealed and urges Jerusalem to put on wedding garments in anticipation of the arrival of her husband (52:1ff.) This same point will be recapitulated in chapters 61 and 62.

One of the repeated themes that appears in this section, as was mentioned in the previous lesson, is the "hand" or "arm" of Yahweh as a metaphor for his mighty power both to judge the evildoer and to deliver those who seek him from the captivity of sin. Here it is found in 51:5, 9, 17, and 52:10.

ONE

I Shall Not Be Put to Shame

Isaiah 50:4–9 *The Lord G*OD *has given me the tongue of a teacher, that I may know how to sustain the weary with a word. Morning by morning he wakens— wakens my ear to listen as those who are taught.* *⁵The Lord G*OD *has opened my ear, and I was not rebellious, I did not turn backward.* *⁶I gave my back to those who struck me, and my cheeks to those who pulled out the beard; I did not hide my face from insult and spitting.*

*⁷The Lord G*OD *helps me; therefore I have not been disgraced; therefore I have set my face like flint, and I know that I shall not be put to shame;* *⁸he who vindicates me is near. Who will contend with me? Let us stand up together. Who are my adversaries? Let them confront me.* *⁹It is the Lord G*OD *who helps me; who will declare me guilty? All of them will wear out like a garment; the moth will eat them up.*

Understanding the Word. There are three themes that ring through this passage of Scripture, and all three are intertwined around a central idea. That central idea is confident obedience. This Servant is a model of one who has no need to defend himself because he is absolutely certain of the call and the care of "[Yahweh] GOD" (vv. 4, 5, 7, 9). Because his God is Yahweh, all this is true. And because Yahweh is God, there is no one who can defeat this Servant.

The first theme is that of the messenger, one who is commissioned to carry a communication. This is a theme that appeared in the first two songs, but is made more explicit here. Yahweh God "wakens [the Servant's] ear" on a daily basis; he teaches the Servant so that the Servant can teach others, especially "the weary": those who are tempted to give up on themselves, and indeed, on life itself. This Servant does not rebel against the commission given him, but willingly accepts it. This fits in precisely with what we hear Christ saying in John 15:15, "I have made known to you everything that I have heard from my Father" (see also John 5:19; 8:28).

The second theme is that of humiliating suffering. It is not just suffering, as striking might be, but suffering that is intended to humiliate, such as pulling out the beard, or spitting on a person. But the Servant says, "I gave my back" and "I did not hide my face" (v. 6). In other words, he surrendered himself to the pain and humiliation willingly. Why would a person do that if he did not have a masochistic streak in him? No answer is given to that question here, but in the fourth song we will learn that the Servant was willing to undergo these things because they are for the sake of the salvation of others. As mentioned in the introduction, we see a progression in the songs in that this suffering is only hinted at in the first and second songs, is mentioned explicitly here, and then expanded upon in the fourth.

The third theme is that of the Servant's absolute reliance upon Yahweh God. This is especially emphasized in verses 7–9. Once again, it is an expansion on a thought that was just touched on in the first song and expanded slightly in the second. The point being emphasized here is that even though the humiliating suffering might certainly look as though the Servant's trust in God had failed him, that will not be the case at all. The Servant's ministry will be successful; he will not be put to shame, the result of failed trust. Rather, it will be those who abused him who will be disgraced. Once again, the congruence of all of this with the experience of Christ is unmistakable.

1. How does confidence in God's faithfulness enable you to dare what you otherwise might not?

2. What is the significance of Jesus' saying that he only spoke those things his Father had said to him?

3. Why did the suffering that brought us salvation also include humiliation?

T W O

I Will Bring Near My Righteousness

Isaiah 50:10–51:5 *Who among you fears the LORD and obeys the voice of his servant, who walks in darkness and has no light, yet trusts in the name of the LORD and relies upon his God? ¹¹But all of you are kindlers of fire, lighters of* *firebrands. Walk in the flame of your fire, and among the brands that you have kindled! This is what you shall have from my hand: you shall lie down in torment.*

⁵¹:¹Listen to me, you that pursue righteousness, you that seek the LORD. Look to the rock from which you were hewn, and to the quarry from which you were dug. ²Look to Abraham your father and to Sarah who bore you; for he was but one when I called him, but I blessed him and made him many. ³For the LORD will comfort Zion; he will comfort all her waste places, and will make her wilderness like Eden, her desert like the garden of the LORD; joy and gladness will be found in her, thanksgiving and the voice of song.

⁴Listen to me, my people, and give heed to me, my nation; for a teaching will go out from me, and my justice for a light to the peoples. ⁵I will bring near my deliverance swiftly, my salvation has gone out and my arms will rule the peoples; the coastlands wait for me, and for my arm they hope.

Understanding the Word. As mentioned in the introduction, the reflections on the third Servant song are especially directed at those who have a desire to please God by living righteous lives (50:10; 51:1, 4, 7). As 50:10 says, many of these people feel that they are groping in darkness. They feel no assurance of their eternal salvation, and often experience a certain weariness, wondering whether it is all worth it. The temptation is to depend on oneself for the light in one's life. That is a deadly option, as 50:11 explains. That fire of self-sufficiency can very easily burn up the ones who light it.

But if the condition just described defines *us*, what should we do? The answer is given in 51:1–5. Two primary points are made. First, the prophet calls on us to remember where we came from, or better, *who* we came from. He points us back to Abraham and Sarah, the ancestors of *the faith* (vv. 1–2). Here is the issue for every one of us. Is righteous living important? Absolutely! Does God want us to live the way the Bible lays out for us? Certainly! *But* righteous living cannot overcome the alienation from God that sin has brought into the world. Why not? Because all our righteous behavior is necessarily tainted with our innate self-centeredness. That is, we are tempted to be good people to prove to God that we are good enough to deserve eternal life. But that is the essence of the sin problem: we can be independent of God and still make ourselves good enough for him without any help from him. Instead, like Abraham, we must believe what God says about our condition: we are hopelessly estranged from him and can never earn our way back to him.

The prophet's second point is, in fact, a continuation of the first one. But instead of pointing back, he now points forward. We must not only believe (accept) what God says about our condition; we must also believe (accept) what he offers as the solution to that condition (vv. 3–5). He encourages ("comfort[s]," see 40:1) us to dare to believe that he can take the wilderness and waste places of our lives and turn them into gardens. What he began with Abraham and Sarah, he plans to extend to the ends of the earth ("the coast-lands"). How will he do that? The clue is in that phrase "justice for a light to the peoples" (v. 4). This necessarily points us to the Servant as described in 42:1–9 and 49:1–12. This is confirmed in verse 5: "I will bring near *my deliverance* [*righteousness*] swiftly . . . for my arm they [wait in] hope." What is God saying? He is saying that it is God's righteousness (as revealed in the Servant Jesus Christ), not ours, that is the hope of the world; it is his mighty arm of grace that is the means whereby we may have eternal light in our lives.

1. Why do many righteous people seem to lack the light of God's hope in their lives?

2. How should God's righteousness and our righteousness relate to each other?

3. Have you ever admitted that you are separated from God by sin, and accepted God's offer of becoming born again through Jesus Christ? If not, why not do it now?

THREE

You Have Forgotten Yahweh, Your Maker

Isaiah 51:13–17, 22 *You have forgotten the* LORD*, your Maker, who stretched out the heavens and laid the foundations of the earth. You fear continually all day long because of the fury of the oppressor, who is bent on destruction. But where is the fury of the oppressor?* [14]*The oppressed shall speedily be released; they shall not die and go down to the Pit, nor shall they lack bread.* [15]*For I am the* LORD *your God, who stirs up the sea so that its waves roar—the* LORD *of hosts is* *his name. ¹⁶I have put my words in your mouth, and hidden you in the shadow of my hand, stretching out the heavens and laying the foundations of the earth, and saying to Zion, "You are my people."*

¹⁷Rouse yourself, rouse yourself! Stand up, O Jerusalem, you who have drunk at the hand of the LORD the cup of his wrath, who have drunk to the dregs the bowl of staggering. . . .

²²Thus says your Sovereign, the LORD, your God who pleads the cause of his people: See, I have taken from your hand the cup of staggering; you shall drink no more from the bowl of my wrath.

Understanding the Word. God had spoken more tenderly in the earlier part of the chapter, but here he speaks more bluntly. Too often our behavior gives the lie to our words, and that is what God is addressing here. The people claim to be the people of God, and yet their lives are ruled by fear and anxiety. What does that mean? It means, says Yahweh, that they have forgotten him. They may call him their Maker, and say that he is the Creator of the universe, but they certainly do not act that way.

We often do not recognize the true implications of our fears. What do they say? They say that Yahweh, the I AM, is not strong enough to deal with them. Thus, for all practical purposes, we have forgotten that he exists. We have had occasion to talk about this feature of the Hebrew language several times earlier. We may say we know something, but if we do not act on that knowledge, we, in fact, do *not* know it. So, if we are ruled by fears, we have forgotten who Yahweh is. We have become practical atheists.

A further implication of our fears results from the fact that in many cases, as here, it is humans, and what they can do to us, that we fear. This is effectively to put humans in the place of God. Jesus spoke about this very pungently when he said that instead of fearing humans, who could kill the body, we should fear God, who could cast both soul and body into hell (Matt. 10:28).

But how can we overcome such fears of humans? We should feed our minds with the truths about God and about reality that are found in his words (Isa. 51:15–16). In short, we ought to spend more time every day in the Scriptures, which tell us that he is indeed the Creator, Yahweh of heaven's armies, who has made us his very own people (see Psalm 56:4, 10–11). Beyond that he is the righteous Judge, who will one day take the cup of his temporary anger out of our hands and put it into the hands of his enemies forever.

1. What are some of the things you fear? Why is this? What practical steps will you take to address them?

2. What do you need to do to remember God in your daily life?

3. What is the importance of the assurance of eternal life as we face our fears?

FOUR
Awake, Awake, O Zion

Isaiah 52:1–6 *Awake, awake, put on your strength, O Zion! Put on your beautiful garments, O Jerusalem, the holy city; for the uncircumcised and the unclean shall enter you no more. ²Shake yourself from the dust, rise up, O captive Jerusalem; loose the bonds from your neck, O captive daughter Zion!*

³For thus says the LORD: You were sold for nothing, and you shall be redeemed without money. ⁴For thus says the Lord GOD: Long ago, my people went down into Egypt to reside there as aliens; the Assyrian, too, has oppressed them without cause. ⁵Now therefore what am I doing here, says the LORD, seeing that my people are taken away without cause? Their rulers howl, says the LORD, and continually, all day long, my name is despised. ⁶Therefore my people shall know my name; therefore in that day they shall know that it is I who speak; here am I.

Understanding the Word. For the third time in this section (50:4–52:12) there is a call to wake up. The first was in 51:9, where the people, encouraged to believe that God can indeed restore them to himself, call on the arm of Yahweh to wake up. But it is not really God who needs to do that. Rather it was the exiles who needed to shake off their apathy and begin to exercise active faith in what God had promised. So in 51:17 it is personified Jerusalem who is told to waken. That call is repeated here in 52:1. Zion (see the commentary that follows) is called upon to put on her best clothes in preparation for the deliverance that is about to come. The holy city itself had been defiled when the unclean, uncircumcised Babylonians had trampled its sacred precincts. Could it ever be restored and purified? God's response is, "Believe it; expect it; prepare for it!" In the same way, the people had become defiled, superficially by being taken into unclean Babylon, but much more on account of their persistent sinning. As Jeremiah said, they were not really circumcised because they were not circumcised at heart (Jer. 9:25–26). Could they be restored to God in the same way the city could? Again God's answer is, "Yes, yes, yes!" But notice the rather shocking directives of verse 2: *they* must rise up from the dust; *they* must "loose the bonds" from their necks. Surely they cannot release themselves, can they? They cannot break the power of their persistent sinning, can they? Here is the mystery of faith, and the wonder of God's valuing of us. We certainly cannot deliver ourselves from either the penalty or the power of sin. On the other hand, if we will not get up from our lethargy and self-pity and denial, and reach out to take hold of the divine hand extended to us, none of that divine grace can reach us. God thinks this much of us, that he invites us to take an active hand with him in the process of salvation.

There are two other, interrelated points that we must consider in this passage. The first is in verses 3–5. As in the previous lesson, Isaiah is using the metaphor of slavery to make his point. Was an impoverished or helpless Yahweh forced to sell his children into slavery, and thus be forced to come up with some hopelessly large sum to buy them back? Of course not! They went into slavery because he sent them there because of their sins, which had resulted in a self-imposed alienation from him. So there is no barrier to Yahweh's doing exactly what his righteous love demands. Just as he brought their ancestors out of Egypt on his own initiative, so he can restore these people to himself from the "Assyria" of their sin. The related point is that the need for deliverance is twofold. The result of the captivity of the people in Babylon and in their sin was that "[Yahweh's] name is despised" (v. 5). That is, the watching world said that Yahweh was not strong enough or great enough to deliver his people from their double captivity. So, if the people, and we, need deliverance back into the arms of God, God needs to deliver us so that the world, and we, will know that he is indeed the I AM, who can do exactly what he says he will do.

1. Why can God's delivering grace not come to a person who will not actively receive it (that is, exercise active faith)?

2. On the other hand, why can we never say that our faith saves us?

3. Why is it important that God's "name" be correctly known in the world? Why is God's desire to be known in the world not an example of divine pride?

FIVE

Go out from There

Isaiah 52:7–12 *How beautiful upon the mountains are the feet of the messenger who announces peace, who brings good news, who announces salvation, who says to Zion, "Your God reigns." ⁸Listen! Your sentinels lift up their voices, together they sing for joy; for in plain sight they see the return of the LORD to Zion. ⁹Break forth together into singing, you ruins of Jerusalem; for the LORD has comforted his people, he has redeemed Jerusalem. ¹⁰The LORD has bared his holy arm before the eyes of all the nations; and all the ends of the earth shall see the salvation of our God.*

¹¹Depart, depart, go out from there! Touch no unclean thing; go out from the midst of it, purify yourselves, you who carry the vessels of the LORD. ¹²For you shall not go out in haste, and you shall not go in flight; for the LORD will go before you, and the God of Israel will be your rear guard.

Understanding the Word. This beautiful poem serves as the climax of the anticipation that has been rising ever since chapter 40, but particularly since the beginning of chapter 49. Chapters 41–48 had made it clear that Yahweh could and would deliver his people from Babylon. But the deeper question was whether he was able to deliver them from the alienation from himself that their sin had necessitated. In 49:1–52:12 he has made it clear that he also can and will do that. We have been told that this restoration to the Father will be made possible through the ministry of the Servant, who was first introduced in 42:1–9. We have not yet been told how the Servant will do that, but *that* he will has been reinforced again and again. Now the prophet uses the imagery of a besieged city to graphically illustrate his point. The city is surrounded by a besieging army. No one can go in or out. Unless the siege is lifted in some way, the people inside will be so reduced by famine and disease that capitulation, with all its attendant horrors, will become inescapable. All seems hopeless. But then one of the watchmen on the walls sees someone running through one of the passes in the mountains that surround the city. He is a herald, shouting the good news that Yahweh is coming, and with him a mighty, relieving army. The besiegers scatter, and shortly Yahweh himself comes into view, and it is as though the ruined city itself breaks into song: we have been delivered! It is as though Yahweh has rolled up his sleeve and has displayed a huge bicep that none can withstand. Somehow, the Servant will make it possible that when the people have been delivered from Babylon, they will also be able to be delivered from the consequences of their sin. Thus, they can return not only to Israel, but also to the arms of the truest Lover in the universe.

In verses 11–12, with the besieging army gone, the people are invited to come out of the city. It is almost impossible to imagine the conditions in a city that had endured a long siege. The unburied corpses of those who had died of disease, the filth and decay, would beggar description. So the prophet is saying that we can leave all that behind, all the guilt and shame, all the condemnation, all the defilement of a life of sin, and step out into light and life, clean air, clean water, and a confident journey home, with Yahweh before us, and the God of Israel behind us, just as the pillar of cloud functioned for the Israelites in the desert. If we do not yet know *how* this will all be possible, *that* it is possible, we confidently believe.

1. Why is imagery more powerful than mere exposition?

2. What are your feelings when you contemplate the imagery of these verses?

3. What is it about sin that is being expressed in the imagery of uncleanness, defilement, disease, and decay?

COMMENTARY NOTES

As I mentioned in the introduction to chapters 48–55, the language in this section, and especially here in chapter 51, continues to be that of deliverance from bondage. However, unlike in chapters 41–48, Babylon is never mentioned, nor is any other specific locality. The reason for this, I believe, is that in these chapters, the prophet is speaking of another kind of bondage, that is, the bondage to sin and its effects. The primary effect is alienation from God. If Israel is restored to its land, but no means is found whereby Israel may be forgiven of its sin, there is hardly a reason to return. That is why the language of "clean" and "unclean" appears here. Yes, perhaps the temple precincts may be reconsecrated and cleansed of the ritual uncleanness that the area had contracted, but what is to be done about the actual uncleanness that the people had contracted through sin? Will they be kept in bondage to that? Will unforgiven sin continue to oppress and destroy them? These chapters answer those questions with a resounding, "No!" God has found a way to forgive the past and empower them for righteous living in the future.

In chapter 51:9 the statement is made that Yahweh was the one "who pierced the dragon." A similar statement also appears in 27:1. What is being said in these places? They are a literary allusion to the myth of origins that was common throughout much of the ancient Near East. (See the commentary on Week Six for a fuller discussion.) In all of these the chief god of a culture was said to have defeated a great sea monster and brought the present world out of that being in some way or another. So here that tale is alluded to as a way of speaking of Yahweh's divine power. However, this is not to say that the Bible is endorsing that myth. In the same way that we might describe a beautiful woman as "a real Venus" without ever believing in the Roman fertility myth, so the Bible is simply using the well-known story for literary effect.

When the Bible uses the term "Zion" for Jerusalem, as it does in 52:1, it is emphasizing the spiritual significance of this location as opposed to its historical or political significance. How the term came to be used in this way is not entirely clear. Originally, it seems to have denoted the hill to the west of David's city across what was later called the Tyropoeon Valley. Hezekiah expanded the walls of Jerusalem to include this hill, and the more idealized usage might have begun at that time. Perhaps it expressed the idea of "greater Jerusalem," and then the more spiritualized connotations followed.

"Zion" connotes such ideas as the presence of God, unbroken fellowship with God, the center of the universe, the final home of God's people, complete security in God, and so forth. The term is very common in the Psalms, Isaiah, Jeremiah, and Micah. It is also frequent in Lamentations to express the terrible irony of what had happened to Zion.

Circumcision is another interesting topic in this passage (52:1). It seems to have been practiced among the West-Semitic peoples who inhabited Canaan and Syria. A slightly different form of the practice was also practiced in Egypt. It was not practiced by the Mesopotamians, apparently, and was particularly abhorred by the Greeks. Whereas it had fertility significance among the other peoples, in the Bible it was a sign of acceptance of God's covenant (Gen. 17:9–14). It particularly expressed the surrender of the control of one's life to God. It is therefore interesting that to be uncircumcised was to be considered unclean. While that may have had some actual physical significance (e.g., if an uncircumcised male did not practice good hygiene), its truer significance was with regard to the spirit. So from early times it was understood that what really needed to bear God's mark was the heart (Deut. 10:16). Genuine uncleanness was not a matter of the body, or a matter of the demonic, as in paganism, but of a spirit not rightly related to God. If the symbol (circumcision of the foreskin) did not reflect the reality (circumcision of the heart), then the symbol was meaningless (the point being made by Jeremiah 9:25–26, and also by Galatians 5:6 and Colossians 2:11). Thus, what is being said here is that sin is to God as dirt is to a white cloth. If we insist on controlling our lives for ourselves, it is as though we have rolled in a pigpen. We can no more live in God's presence than dirt can remain in the presence of strong bleach. The occurrence of this language in the conclusion of this section (52:1, 11) is one more evidence that we are not here talking about a physical deliverance, but a spiritual one.

WEEK TEN

GATHERING DISCUSSION OUTLINE

A. Open session in prayer.

B. View video for this week's readings.

C. What general impressions and thoughts do you have after considering the video and reading the daily writings on these scriptures?

D. Discuss questions selected from the daily readings.

1. **KEY OBSERVATION:** The Servant was able to endure humiliating suffering because of his confidence in God's faithfulness.

    DISCUSSION QUESTION: How does confidence in God's faithfulness enable you to dare what you otherwise might not?

2. **KEY OBSERVATION:** It is possible to be living a very righteous life and yet lack the kind of confidence and hope in God that give light to life.

    DISCUSSION QUESTION: Why do many righteous people seem to lack the light of God's hope in their lives?

3. **KEY OBSERVATION:** When we allow our fears to control our thinking, we have effectively forgotten God.

    DISCUSSION QUESTION: What do you need to do to remember God in your daily life?

4. **KEY OBSERVATION:** God's free salvation is ineffective in our lives unless we actively receive it.

   DISCUSSION QUESTION: Why can God's delivering grace not come to a person who will not actively receive it (that is, exercise active faith)?

5. **KEY OBSERVATION:** God has come to us in Christ to deliver us from the defilement and captivity of sin.

   DISCUSSION QUESTION: What is it about sin that is being expressed in the imagery of uncleanness, defilement, disease, and decay?

E. What facts and information presented in the commentary portion of the lesson help you understand the weekly scripture?

F. Close session with prayer.

WEEK ELEVEN

Isaiah 52:13–53:12

The Suffering Servant

INTRODUCTION

Like few other passages in the Bible, this one has remarkable literary and theological power. Christians have always held it in special reverence because, on the force of the New Testament (see Acts 8:26–35), we have understood it to be referring to Christ. But even without that special appeal, interpreters have been fascinated by it. It stands out like Psalm 23, or Isaiah 6, or 1 Corinthians 13 as a unique and powerful piece of literature. In five three-verse stanzas it paints an unforgettable picture of one who, though calling little attention to himself, nevertheless gives his life in a way that has universal impact. Those who deny the connection with Christ have a very difficult time finding some other figure, whether human or divine, to replace him.

All this being so, it is somewhat ironic that the chapter division has separated the first stanza of the poem (52:13–15) from the rest, situating it at the end of chapter 52. But there is no doubt that the chapter division is incorrect. The content clearly goes with the rest of what is now chapter 53. That mix-up need not trouble us since the chapter divisions were only put in during the first millennium after Christ, long after the Old Testament was complete. It is more of a question why someone would have put the chapter division there, but there is no settled answer to the question.

The poem begins and ends on a note of triumph. In 52:13 we are assured that the Servant's ministry will be successful and that he will be highly exalted. Then in 53:12 we see the Servant as the victor, dividing the spoils of the battle. But between these two high points, there is almost unbelievable loss. The responses to the Servant move from astonishment to dismissal and rejection to judicial murder. His suffering is seen as being his own fault, even though in fact none of it was deserved. He suffers so that others (we!) can be healed. He is deprived of justice, and of the two markers of a successful life in the ancient world, old age and many children. Perhaps worst of all, all of this is orchestrated by God. Nevertheless, the Servant's suffering and death will be the means whereby we may be declared innocent ("justified") before God and be made right with him. The Servant is the means whereby Israel and, indeed, the whole world, may become servants of the holy God.

ONE

Exalted, Yet Shocking

Isaiah 52:13–15 *See, my servant shall prosper; he shall be exalted and lifted up, and shall be very high.* [14]*Just as there were many who were astonished at him—so marred was his appearance, beyond human semblance, and his form beyond that of mortals—*[15]*so he shall startle many nations; kings shall shut their mouths because of him; for that which had not been told them they shall see, and that which they had not heard they shall contemplate.*

Understanding the Word. As noted earlier, the poem begins with assertions about the certain success of the Servant's mission. Two things are said about this in verse 13. First, it is flatly stated that he will be successful. If you look at other translations, some will say that he will be wise, and others say he will be prudent, whereas those in the NRSV tradition say he will prosper. This is a matter of the Hebrew word being used here (and again in 53:10, which we will discuss momentarily). See the commentary that follows for a fuller discussion, but let it be said here that the basic idea of the word is to be effective, with the other connotations stemming from and depending on the particular context where the word occurs. But this verse is *not* saying that the Servant will become wealthy, or even that he will be a wise man. It is saying that in spite of all the difficulties, hardships, and downright tragedy that is going to be unfolded in the following verses, he *will* succeed in what he is sent to do. This same thought is found in all three of the preceding Servant poems (42:4; 49:4; 50:7–9). It was obviously a vital thought to the Servant. How necessary this confidence must have been when people and disciples alike seemed incapable of grasping what he had come to do.

The second point that is made in verse 13 follows on the first. Since he will be successful in the end, he is going to receive due recognition for accomplishing that incredible work of making it possible for the entire race to be restored to God. He will be given the highest place. But there is something more hidden here: the words "lifted up" and "very high" occur in two other places in the book, and both of them refer to God! The first occurrence is in 6:1: "I saw [Yahweh] sitting on a throne, *high and [lifted up]*" (NRSV "lofty") (emphasis added). The second is in 57:15: "Thus says *the high and [lifted up]* (NRSV "lofty") one, who inhabits eternity, whose name is holy" (emphasis added). Now here we have the third occurrence. Can you imagine Isaiah scratching his head and saying, "*What* did I just say?! Is the Servant God?! How can that be?!" We are privileged to know the answer (see 1 Peter 1:10–11).

But from those heights, we immediately start the descent. Verses 14 and 15 speak of the astonishment that the Servant and his ministry were going to cause. Did we wish for a uniformed drum major to lead our triumphal parade back to God? No? Perhaps, like the Jews, we were looking for someone who would prove to the world that we really are God's favorites. But not this man! It has been said that in the modern world it is impossible for a truly ugly person to be elected to high office. Abraham Lincoln would have no chance today. Yet this man did not look at all like the deliverer that was expected. The marred face may refer to the crucifixion, but it may also be metaphorical to speak of the startling (see the commentary) manner by which the deliverance from sin's alienation would be accomplished. Surely that deliverance required power, like the power of beauty, not weakness.

1. What were some of the aspects of Jesus' ministry that were startling and astonishing to the people of his day?

2. What did knowing how the story ends mean for Jesus in what he was called upon to endure in his earthly life? How does it enable us to endure hard times in our Christian walk?

3. What are some of the most important aspects of Christ's deity for you?

TWO

Who Can Believe It?

Isaiah 53:1–3 *Who has believed what we have heard? And to whom has the arm of the LORD been revealed? ²For he grew up before him like a young plant, and like a root out of dry ground; he had no form or majesty that we should look at him, nothing in his appearance that we should desire him. ³He was despised and rejected by others; a man of suffering and acquainted with infirmity; and as one from whom others hide their faces he was despised, and we held him of no account.*

Understanding the Word. In this stanza the theme of astonishment continues on from the previous one and ultimately leads to outright rejection. It is certainly possible to understand how these attitudes could have arisen. After all, in the previous chapters, with their emphasis on the mighty arm of Yahweh, one could certainly be forgiven for expecting an obvious manifestation of power displayed in the overthrow of sin. And when the twenty-seven-inch bicep that we had been looking for turns out to be a spindly-looking thing that would apparently have difficulty removing a cupcake paper, we could be pardoned for thinking this was not what we needed. Indeed, the prophet is at some pains to make his point about the unassuming appearance of the Servant. He does not burst on the scene with a mighty fanfare, and he does not sweep through the earth in triumph, looking like a young Adonis. Instead, his arrival on the scene will be as quiet as a plant's coming up, and his progress will be as indiscernible as that of a plant growing in dry soil. As for his appearance, as already pointed out, there was nothing about it to draw people to him. He probably did not have the serene beauty of Sallman's *Head of Christ* that many of us knew in childhood. If he would draw people, as he most certainly did, it would have to be something other than the trappings of power and beauty.

In Christ's life, it is apparent that it was the power to do miracles that attracted the crowds to him in his early ministry. But as the crowds began to listen more carefully to what he actually said, things like the son of the owner of the vineyard being killed by the tenants of the vineyard, and cutting off your hand if it led you into sin, they began to drift away. And when he actually began to talk about eating his body and drinking his blood, they hurried away.

Twice in verse 3 we are told that the Servant was "despised." While the Hebrew word can have the overtone of contempt that is characteristic of the English word, the basic idea is simply to consider worthless. Something that is despised is simply not worthy of attention. Clearly the priests despised Jesus with the full range of contempt. But ordinary people simply ended up dismissing this man as a bit of a humbug, rejecting him and his strange pronouncements as unworthy of their attention.

There has been some uncertainty about the precise sense of the middle part of verse 3. The classic King James translation says, "a man of sorrows, and acquainted with grief." The NRSV that is used here is a bit more literal when it says "a man of suffering and acquainted with infirmity." But a completely literal translation would be "a man of pain and acquainted with sickness." When that is coupled with the following turning away of the face, it has suggested to some that a leper is being depicted. I suspect that is correct, but that the prophet is speaking figuratively. Far from being someone to whom people would be superficially attracted, the Servant is someone from whom people would instinctively turn away. It is frankly embarrassing for someone to be openly transparent with us, for someone to make no effort to protect himself or herself from the hurts of the world, but to actually invite them. If that is the road of servanthood, most of us would rather try some other.

1. How did Jesus differ from the expectations of the Jewish people, and what does his example say about our lives and ministries?

2. Jesus is often referred to as a "good teacher." But several things Jesus said, like those mentioned in this day's study, are frankly unsettling, ones we might like to dismiss. What are some of his other unsettling sayings you can think of?

3. What are some of the ways you and I are tempted to despise Jesus (think him not worthy of our attention)?

THREE

Wounded for Our Transgressions

Isaiah 53:4–6 *Surely he has borne our infirmities and carried our diseases; yet we accounted him stricken, struck down by God, and afflicted. ⁵But he was wounded for our transgressions, crushed for our iniquities; upon him was the punishment that made us whole, and by his bruises we are healed. ⁶All we like sheep have gone astray; we have all turned to our own way, and the LORD has laid on him the iniquity of us all.*

Understanding the Word. Here the poet moves from speaking of the result of servanthood—astonishment and rejection—to the burden of servanthood. In doing so, he masterfully connects the two stanzas. In the previous stanza he said that the Servant was a man of pain, acquainted with sickness. Now he asks, "Whose pain? Whose sickness?" The answer, in verse 4, is the shocking, "Ours."

"Certainly not," we answer. "He brought this on himself." Or maybe more than that, maybe God was punishing him for his heretical teachings about himself, and for his hostile treatment of those good men, the priests, the teachers of the law, and the Pharisees. "Certainly you can't blame us. He brought all this on himself; he had it coming to him." But the prophet will have none of that. You might want to mark the first-person pronouns in verses 5 and 6. It is all about "our," "we," and "us," isn't it? If the Servant has contracted moral leprosy, from whom did he get it? He got it from us. His illness is our illness. Here is a picture of the seriousness of sin. It cannot be removed with a few nice words or bit of ritual. It is as deadly as cancer. Somehow it must be taken from us, and the only way for that to happen is for another to take it upon himself. Then Isaiah changes the metaphor from sickness to abuse. We deserve to be whipped for what we have done to the Creator. But no, the Servant gets whipped, and we not only escape the whipping; we get healed in the process (see the commentary for KJV "peace"). The "welts" on our backs—all the psychological and emotional and even physical damages that have come as a result of our attempts to live life our own way—get healed and we are made whole because he has taken all the damage onto himself.

Then the poet changes the metaphor once more. We are like sheep, he says. Some say that sheep are stupid. My father and I raised sheep, and I am not sure they are as stupid as they are single-minded. They move from one delicious clump of grass to another without paying much attention to their surroundings, until all of a sudden they find themselves in some strange place they have never been before. How like us. We simply want what we want when we want it, and one day find ourselves enslaved to our desires, surrounded by a lot of outdated stuff that we secretly wonder why we ever bought. The English word to translate that condition is "iniquity." It is unfortunate that we have no good modern equivalent for that word, because it is a very important concept. Like most Hebrew concepts, it is very wide-ranging. The fundamental idea seems to be twistedness, and it can refer to both our situation and the cause of our situation. It is because of our twisted view of God and the world and ourselves that we end up in a completely twisted-up situation. What is God's response to this mess? Does he shriek at us, or wipe his hands of us? No, he lays the whole thing on the back of his Servant, who, like the goat on the Day of Atonement, carries it all away outside the camp (Lev. 16:20–22).

1. What is it about the nature of cause and effect that makes it impossible for God simply to ignore sin? Why must its effects be carried by someone?

2. In what ways do we attempt to deny our responsibility for our sins?

3. What is the evidence of iniquity in some of our attitudes toward God, the world, and ourselves?

FOUR

By a Perversion of Justice He Was Taken Away

Isaiah 53:7–9 *He was oppressed, and he was afflicted, yet he did not open his mouth; like a lamb that is led to the slaughter, and like a sheep that before its shearers is silent, so he did not open his mouth. ⁸By a perversion of justice he was taken away. Who could have imagined his future? For he was cut off from the land of the living, stricken for the transgression of my people. ⁹They made* *his grave with the wicked and his tomb with the rich, although he had done no violence, and there was no deceit in his mouth.*

Understanding the Word. In this stanza we move from the burden of servanthood to the outcome of servanthood. Once again, the poet masterfully ties the two stanzas together. Here he does so with the continuation of the sheep metaphor. What does "sheepliness" look like in us? It is that mild stubborn willfulness that says, "I will satisfy my needs as I choose, and I don't care about anything else." But what does the sheep nature look like when the Servant takes it upon himself? Now it is that complete defenselessness that characterizes all sheep. He does not seek to defend himself; he does not bleat about the unfairness of it all; he simply goes quietly to his doom—for us.

Unfairness, yes, that is the word that seems to summarize the apparent outcome of this selfless service. You would think that if there is a scrap of justice in the world, the outcome of service like this would be some sort of gratitude. But no, it is not to be. He is taken away by oppression and injustice. A number of books have been written on the manifest injustice of Jesus' "trial" before the high council of the Jews (see Matthew 26:57–68) and before the Roman governor, Pilate (see Matthew 27:11–26). The NRSV phrase here, "a perversion of justice" (Isa. 53:8), is very apt. But there is more to it than this. The Servant is not even allowed the dignity of a life well lived. In Old Testament times the marks of such a life were old age and many children. This Servant is denied both. He has no future (posterity) because the string of his life is cut off right in the middle (for the link between "cut off" and "posterity," see Psalms 37:38; 109:13). But the unfairness is not ended. When the Servant is deprived of justice and killed while still young, he is not even permitted the favor of being buried with the poor, whom he loved, but is put down among the wicked rich. The Old Testament attitude toward riches is very ambiguous. If you are a righteous person, and attain riches, that is a blessing from God, and if you use your riches to assist the poor, you are doubly blessed. But sadly, in most cases, says the Old Testament, rich people have gotten their riches through oppression, injustice, and treachery, and use it for themselves alone. That is the sense here. Even though the Servant had never done the things ("violence" and "deceit") that the dead rich all around him had done, he was still buried among them. This is a classic example of adding insult to injury.

As we saw in all three of the previous Servant Songs, the Servant recognized with increasing clarity that the apparent outcome of his service was going to be failure, and not only failure, but failure in the midst of abuse and mistreatment. Knowing that to be the case, how could he go on? How could he set his face to go to Jerusalem when he knew it would all end in humiliating failure? And it would. How humiliating to be hanging there, naked, gasping for just one more breath, while the high priest and his fellows mocked you and dared you to do what you could not do and be faithful to the Father, come down off the cross and give those guys what they had coming to them? The only way he was able to do that was that, long ago, he had committed the outcome of his service to his Father. His calling was to be faithful; the outcome was up to the Father. The Father had assured him that in spite of appearances, the ultimate outcome would be glory in a redeemed world, but that was the Father's business. The Servant's task was very simple: be faithful and leave the outcome to the Father.

1. When we demand to see an immediate good outcome from our service, what does that say about us and our motivation?

2. Why do you think there was so much unfairness clustered around Jesus at the end of his life?

3. What benefits accrue to us when we are genuinely able to leave the outcome of our service in our Father's hands?

FIVE

Redemptive Suffering

Isaiah 53:10–12 *Yet it was the will of the LORD to crush him with pain. When you make his life an offering for sin, he shall see his offspring, and shall prolong his days; through him the will of the LORD shall prosper. [11]Out of his anguish he shall see light; he shall find satisfaction through his knowledge. The righteous one, my servant, shall make many righteous, and he shall bear their iniquities. [12]Therefore I will allot him a portion with the great, and he shall divide the spoil with the strong; because he poured out himself to death, and was numbered with the transgressors; yet he bore the sin of many, and made intercession for the transgressors.*

Understanding the Word. Once again, the prophet carries us from the previous stanza into this one where he discusses what really issued from the Servant's ministry. He does so by answering an implicit question that previous stanza raised: Why would the Father allow such an unfair outcome? The answer, as given here, is a frightening one: the Father wanted to do it (the Hebrew term conveys more than the mere neutral "will"; "wanted to" comes closer). Our immediate response is, "Surely not!" What father, except a deranged one, would want to see his son tortured to death? Before we go further here, we must lay to rest a slander that unbelievers (some of them Christian clergy) have passed off on Christian doctrine. They have said that orthodox Christian faith has sanctioned child abuse by suggesting that the Father sacrifices the Son. Almost all who say these kinds of things know better. The Christian doctrine of the Trinity never endorses the sort of disconnection of one person of the Trinity from another that this statement assumes. It is God—Father, Son, and Spirit—who die all together for the sins of the world. To suggest that one divine person forces another divine person to do something he did not want to do is almost blasphemy. If we in the limitations of our language express the manner of the functioning of the Godhead in Father/Son language, we must never think for one moment that the whole of the Godhead was not involved in the sacrifice of the Son.

But why did Yahweh want to sacrifice the Servant? The answer is given in the next sentence: so you and I might be provided with a sin offering. The realization that there is something amiss between us and whatever deity we conceive of as running this world is ingrained in every human being. This is why, around the world, people sense a need to do something to make certain that "the gods" are favorable to them. And again, around the world, the sense is that only blood sacrifice will accomplish that. But it is only in the Bible that a comprehensive explanation for this instinct is given, and likewise, a comprehensive solution is found. Clearly, as the prophet Micah understood, the blood of bulls and goats, and even of one's own child, is not enough to cover the death penalty for one's own sin (Mic. 6:6–7). What is to be done? Could we imagine some other solution than this one? Perhaps. But the fact is, this one is astonishingly complete: God becomes a man, thus incurring our human liability to sin. But that man does not sin, thus making it possible for him to take the death of another upon himself. And since this man is God, he can take the death of *all* others upon himself. Had he not become a man, he would not be liable to sin, and if he had not retained his deity, he could not have died for all. Thus, when you and I, admit that we need a sin offering, accept what he had done for us, and symbolically offer him up to the Father, the reason Yahweh wanted to do this will succeed ("prosper"), the one who was cut off in midlife without children will see millions of offspring, and will live forever. The tragedy would be if you and I, secure in our self-righteousness, were to say, "I certainly don't need any sin offering." Then the whole thing would be for nothing. But as it is, having borne the sins of many, he has made many righteous. The issue of this servanthood is redemption.

1. We tend to think of the death penalty for sin as being cruel and unusual punishment, something arbitrarily imposed by a cruel God. But think of the analogy of jumping off a tall building and the death that results. Is that result cruel, unusual, and arbitrary? Why not? How does this help us understand the death penalty for sin?

2. It might be argued that we don't know before we do it that sin results in "the second death"—eternal separation from God, and that, therefore, it is unfair to impose that result upon us. But suppose a baby falls from a thirtieth-floor window? Can ignorance suspend cause and effect?

3. Continuing the analogy of falling from a tall building, what has God done for us through the Servant?

COMMENTARY NOTES

In the Hebrew Bible there are section and paragraph markers that the Jewish scholars of the first century after Christ have added. These are not inspired, but they are often helpful. In the case of this passage, there is a break indicated between 52:12 and and 52:13 and another between 53:12 and 54:1. This shows us that these scholars understood 52:13 to 53:12 to be a single unit, as I mentioned earlier.

A note on phrasing: the traditional rendering (KJV) of 52:15a is, "So shall he sprinkle many nations." It is completely understandable why the King James translators would choose this translation since the only word in the Hebrew vocabulary with these particular consonants means "to sprinkle." This wording has been particularly appreciated by Christians who think of the parallel between Christ's blood and the blood of the sacrificial animal that was "sprinkled" on the altar as well as the ark of the covenant (Lev. 16:14).

However, there are two strong arguments against this translation. The first is in the nature of Hebrew poetry. It is not characterized by rhyme or meter, but by what has come to be called *parallelism*. That is, the same thought is expressed in two successive clauses, but in synonyms, as for instance in this hypothetical example: "God founded the earth; Yahweh stretched out the heavens." Together the two clauses are speaking of God as Creator. Here, the second clause

is "kings shall shut their mouths at him" (KJV). There is no way to make that synonymous with "So shall he sprinkle many nations."

The other problem is that in all of the other occurrences of the word (there are not many), the object of the verb is sprinkled on something. That would argue that in this case the Servant is going to sprinkle many nations onto something else, a clearly nonsensical idea.

The Greek translation of the Old Testament, called the Septuagint, has, "He amazed many nations," and when it was discovered that there is a word with these consonants in Arabic meaning "to startle," the solution to the problem seemed clear. The sentence actually says (as in NRSV, and similarly in the NLT), "He shall startle many nations; kings will shut their mouths because of him." Other modern translations have resisted this change, partly because of tradition, but also because this would be the only occurrence of this word in the Bible. However, Hebrew poetry is notorious for utilizing rare words that do not occur elsewhere, so this fact need not be a barrier to correcting a mistaken translation.

On that note, as I have said several times previously, biblical Hebrew has a very small vocabulary. This means that many Hebrew words have a very large pool of meanings, and that the translator needs to be very conscious of the given context in order to choose the correct translation in that case.

We have an example of the problem here in 52:13 and again in 53:10. It is the word conventionally translated "prosper." In certain contexts that is the correct rendering, but the word can also be translated, "to be wise," or, "to be prudent." What do these meanings have in common? The common idea is "to be effective." If you are to be effective, you must be wise and prudent; and if you are effective, then you will reap the results of that accomplishment. In short, you will prosper. The modern equivalent that best applies here, as I said earlier, is "to be successful." At the very outset of the poem, with its descriptions of the very grave consequences the Servant will face, we the readers are assured that he *will* succeed in the work to which he is called. Our hearts need not quail as we read. In the same way, we are told in 53:10 that when we make the Servant a sin offering, then what Yahweh intended in this ordeal will be gloriously successful. "Prosper," with its current English connotation of "to become rich," almost completely obscures the point.

Looking next at 52:14, the Hebrew of that verse says, "Just as many were astonished at you, so marred was his appearance . . ." Who this "you" might be is a problem, because there is no identification in the text. The Greek Septuagint and the Latin Vulgate both have "you," while the Syriac and the Aramaic Targum have "him." This latter translation has been adopted by several of the modern English versions, even though the latter two witnesses are not very strong. In the Hebrew "you" and "him" are each represented by only one letter, and the two are quite similar, so an error of the eye is possible. If "you" is correct, then possibly it is a reference to the prophet, who for some reason may have had a disfigurement.

In the next chapter, the NRSV "upon him was the punishment that made us whole" (see also NLT: "He was beaten so we could be whole") has better captured the sense of 53:5 than does the traditional rendering, "the chastisement of our peace was upon him," which is unfortunately almost completely without meaning. The problem is with the word translated "peace." It is a problem very similar to that of "prosper" discussed earlier. The consonants *sh l m* have a wide range of meaning, with an underlying idea of "wholeness." So wholeness between peoples or nations can be described as "peace," but wholeness in the body is "health," and that is clearly the sense here. The Servant suffers the ill health resulting from a beating so that we can experience the health of not being beaten.

Many scholars resist any connection between the Servant and Jesus Christ on the basis of their resistance to the possibility of predictive prophecy, especially a prediction that would have been given anywhere from seven hundred to five hundred years in advance. Since we have already discussed this issue, we will not go into it any further here. But if Christ is not a possibility, then what is the alternative? Here is where the real difficulty emerges. If this is a person contemporary with the so-called Second Isaiah of 545 BC, as most of these scholars would insist, who is it? What ordinary human died for the sins of the nations in 545 BC? "Second Isaiah" himself? Some unknown leper? Jeremiah? The lengths to which these people must go (including denying that the Servant actually died) to support their hypotheses argues that, in fact, there is no reasonable alternative who is contemporary with either the historical Isaiah or the hypothetical "Second Isaiah."

Next, in the translations of 53:10 we see a parade example of the force of Christian doctrine over accurate translation. The Hebrew says "when you make him an offering for sin," but apart from the King James Version and the NRSV, virtually all other translations alter the plain sense of the text. The most obvious sense of "you" is the hearer/reader. When we make the Servant a sin offering, certain results follow. But that suggests that we humans have a part to play in our salvation. But according to certain forms of Christian doctrine, we humans are completely passive in the process, we only receive what God has done. Thus, the text *should* say something else, and that is in fact what the translators do, although they do not agree on exactly how the text should be altered. So we have:

- "when his soul makes an offering for guilt" (ESV)
- "If He would render Himself *as* a guilt offering" (NASB)
- "and though the LORD makes his life an offering for sin" (NIV)
- "Yet when his life is made an offering for sin" (NLT)
- "When You [God] make His soul an offering for sin" (NKJV)

My question is, why not make our doctrine conform to the text instead of making the text conform to our doctrine? The text does not say that we save ourselves, but it does say that we have to respond in faith to what God has done.

WEEK ELEVEN

GATHERING DISCUSSION OUTLINE

A. Open session in prayer.

B. View video for this week's readings.

C. What general impressions and thoughts do you have after considering the video and reading the daily writings on these scriptures?

D. Discuss questions selected from the daily readings.

> **1.** **KEY OBSERVATION:** The work of the Servant begins and ends in triumph.
>
> **DISCUSSION QUESTION:** What did knowing how the story ends mean for Jesus in what he was called upon to endure in his earthly life? How does it enable us to endure hard times in our Christian walk?

> **2.** **KEY OBSERVATION:** When Jesus appeared, he was not at all what people expected him to be.
>
> **DISCUSSION QUESTION:** How did Jesus differ from the expectations, and what does his example say about our lives and ministries?

> **3.** **KEY OBSERVATION:** The Servant had to carry our sins, iniquity, and transgressions.
>
> **DISCUSSION QUESTION:** What is it about the nature of cause and effect that makes it impossible for God simply to ignore sin? Why must its effects be carried by someone?

4. **KEY OBSERVATION:** The immediate outcome of the Servant's ministry was injustice and oppression on every level.

   DISCUSSION QUESTION: Why do you think there was so much unfairness clustered around Jesus at the end of his life?

   5. **KEY OBSERVATION:** The ultimate issue of the Servant's ministry was redemption for multitudes. Christ has died in our place.

   DISCUSSION QUESTION: If sin is analogous to jumping off a tall building, with death the necessary result, then on that same analogy, what has God done for us in Christ?

E. What facts and information presented in the commentary portion of the lesson help you understand the weekly scripture?

F. Close session with prayer.

WEEK TWELVE

Isaiah 54:1–55:13

Come to the Waters

INTRODUCTION

In these two chapters we come to the invitation to experience all that the Servant has accomplished for his people. The language is highly emotive and figurative, but it is particularly focused on the restored relationship with Yahweh. Israel has been like a widow who has lost all her children. Now she finds herself back with her husband and with more children from the relationship than she could ever imagine. We have encountered this fear before that the line of Israel, both in the flesh and in the faith, would disappear, but now Israel is assured that her children will reach around the world.

Who is this husband who welcomes her back? Is he some primitive local deity, an idol made with human hands? No, he is the Maker, Yahweh of heaven's armies (NRSV, "the Lord of hosts"), the Holy One of Israel, the Redeemer, the God of the whole earth (54:5). His anger with her was but for a moment, but his unfailing love for her is eternal. And the love is not a kind of formal, judicial thing, but characterized through and through with tender compassion. So God promises that from his side, his bride is secure for all eternity. In that light he invites her to come and enjoy all the blessings that she had worked so fruitlessly to produce for herself, blessings that would now result from a covenant growing out of Yahweh's love for David (55:3). The result would be the fulfillment of the promise made all the way back in chapter 2: the nations will come to Jerusalem because of Yahweh, their God. Finally, God implores them to receive his forgiveness and restoration that the Servant made possible, even if they do not quite understand the mechanism of all that. Don't miss it, he says, because here is eternal joy not only for humans, but for the whole cosmos.

ONE

Sing, O Barren One

Isaiah 54:1–4 *Sing, O barren one who did not bear; burst into song and shout, you who have not been in labor! For the children of the desolate woman will be more than the children of her that is married, says the* LORD. *²Enlarge the site of your tent, and let the curtains of your habitations be stretched out; do not hold back; lengthen your cords and strengthen your stakes. ³For you will spread out to the right and to the left, and your descendants will possess the nations and will settle the desolate towns.*

⁴Do not fear, for you will not be ashamed; do not be discouraged, for you will not suffer disgrace; for you will forget the shame of your youth, and the disgrace of your widowhood you will remember no more.

Understanding the Word. These four verses are the first half of a unit that extends through verse 10. They are addressed to the exiles, who are personified as a childless widow. The theme of the barren woman is a recurring one in the Scriptures, especially in Genesis 12–30. The first three "mothers of Israel"—Sarah, Rebekah, and Rachel—were all unable to have children. This was in the face of Yahweh's great promise to Abraham that he would have more descendants than the stars of the heavens or the sands of the seashore. But this concern for children was not something that was restricted to the Bible; it was the burning concern of the entire ancient world. This was the reason for the popularity of the various pagan fertility cults. To die without having had children was not only a social disgrace; it was clearly a sign of divine disfavor showing that the deity wanted to cut off your family line. As I said in the previous lesson, that seemed to be the case with the Servant, although in fact, because of his obedience, he has children around the world. But there was also a very practical reason for wanting many children: it was one of the surest ways to some degree of wealth and comfort. Sons could work larger areas of farmland, and daughters could be married to neighbors whose land would add to your own.

But the biblical point is that many children are not the result of a couple's own virility and fecundity, much less their involvement in fertility rituals. Rather, they are the result of the undeserved grace of God, lavished on those who will stop trying to manipulate his power, but will live in faithful trust in him. So it was in every one of those first three generations: children are the gift of God, not the product of human strength or of human manipulation. Of course, the point that Yahweh is making is true for all of life. As I said earlier, this does not mean that we simply sit passively, waiting for God to drop his good gifts upon us. God thinks too much of us for that. He wants us, as any good father does, to have the joy of accomplishment as we work beside him. But we must never think that it is our strength, or our intelligence, or our cunning that makes life rich and meaningful. To go down that road is to be led badly astray (see Isaiah 47:10).

Here, Judah is tempted to give up hope. Her land is gone, her ancient heritage of faith seems to have been canceled out by recent events, her descendants are likely to abandon everything that has defined the Israelite culture, and her sins have finally separated her from her God, her "husband," forever. She is truly barren, and all that she has loved and believed in will die with her. What a wonder then when Yahweh says that she is going to have more children than she can count, that her tent will not be big enough to hold them all, and that they will spread out in every direction! How can this be? The answer lies in the preceding chapter. Through the Servant, God has found a way to satisfy the demands of his justice and can take his Beloved back into his arms again without his holiness destroying her in the process.

1. Where would you say the line is between our merely trying to supply our needs for ourselves, and trusting God to supply our needs?

2. How does Christ's suffering make it possible for God to take us in his arms and not have his holiness destroy us?

3. What are some of the best ways for us to pass the heritage of our faith to the rising generation?

TWO

Your Maker Is Your Husband

Isaiah 54:5–10 *For your Maker is your husband, the* LORD *of hosts is his name; the Holy One of Israel is your Redeemer, the God of the whole earth he is called.* ⁶*For the* LORD *has called you like a wife forsaken and grieved in spirit, like the* *wife of a man's youth when she is cast off, says your God. ⁷For a brief moment I abandoned you, but with great compassion I will gather you. ⁸In overflowing wrath for a moment I hid my face from you, but with everlasting love I will have compassion on you, says the LORD, your Redeemer.*

⁹This is like the days of Noah to me: Just as I swore that the waters of Noah would never again go over the earth, so I have sworn that I will not be angry with you and will not rebuke you. ¹⁰For the mountains may depart and the hills be removed, but my steadfast love shall not depart from you, and my covenant of peace shall not be removed, says the LORD, who has compassion on you.

Understanding the Word. Verses 1–4 told us what the effect was: many, many children. Now in verses 5–10 we learn what is the cause that produced such an effect. We can recognize this by the "For" that begins verse 5: "Sing . . . let the curtains of your habitations be stretched out. . . . For . . ." (vv. 1–2, 5). What is that cause? Above everything else, the cause for the invitation lies in the character and nature of God. I pointed out in the introduction the piling up of names and titles for God in verse 5. These names and titles stress his creatorship, his universal power, his holiness, his immanence, *and* that he is *your Redeemer.* That is, he has the authority and the power and the desire to restore his people to himself in spite of their sin. This being so, Israel need not fear as to whether the ancient promises will have failed.

The following verses, 6–10, flesh out this claim, beginning with another "For" in verse 6. Israel has reason for hope because, although God had divorced Israel, he now has taken her back to himself. In the Torah (Deut. 24:3–4), if a divorced woman has subsequently had relations with another man, the first husband may not take her back. Here there is no indication of such a subsequent relationship, but see Hosea 3:1–3, where the prophet is specifically commanded to take his wife back when there had been such an instance, because, God says, that is what Israel had done. In short, God's love transcends the limits of the law, which had only been designed to restrain evil.

As the subsequent verses continue to explore how Yahweh's nature and character are the cause of Israel's rejoicing, they emphasize another point that the book of Hosea makes: God's anger is temporary, but his love is eternal. Therefore, when he permits judgment to come upon us, its purpose is not destruction, but refining. So he says to Israel that he will not destroy her (as she deserves), because he is not man, but God (Hosea 11:9). We may say it this way: God *gets* angry, but he *is* love. The same point is made in Psalm 30:5, which says, "His anger lasts only a moment, but his favor lasts a lifetime" (NIV). His "overflowing wrath" is no match for his "everlasting love." This love is not merely affection or passion, but the determination of a superior to do good to an inferior, even if, or perhaps *especially* if, it is undeserved. (For more on *hesed* as self-giving, self-denying love, see the commentary that follows.) It expresses itself in compassion, that ability to feel with another and to take action in accord with that feeling. The supreme example of God's compassion is found in the incarnation, the "enfleshment," of Jesus Christ. Here God became one of us, experiencing what we experience. That was compassion "with skin on," as a child expressed it.

What does "everlasting love" entail? Verses 9 and 10 address that question. Will God ever break his promises to his people? He will no more do that than break his promise to Noah about not destroying the earth with a flood again. Are his *hesed* and his *shalom* variable? No, they are more certain than the mountains and the hills. (On the relation of these promises to historical events, see the commentary that follows.)

1. What are some specific ways in which the incarnation of Christ expresses Yahweh's compassion?

2. In what ways have you experienced the truth that God's anger is for a moment, but his favor is for a lifetime?

3. Consider how the charge "Let us love, not in word or speech, but in truth and action" (1 John 3:18) relates to the meaning of *hesed* as love.

THREE
I Will Make Your Pinnacles of Rubies

Isaiah 54:11–17 *O afflicted one, storm-tossed, and not comforted, I am about to set your stones in antimony, and lay your foundations with sapphires. ¹²I will make your pinnacles of rubies, your gates of jewels, and all your wall of precious stones. ¹³All your children shall be taught by the LORD, and great shall be the prosperity of your children. ¹⁴In righteousness you shall be established; you shall be far from oppression, for you shall not fear; and from terror, for it shall not* *come near you. ¹⁵If anyone stirs up strife, it is not from me; whoever stirs up strife with you shall fall because of you. ¹⁶See it is I who have created the smith who blows the fire of coals, and produces a weapon fit for its purpose; I have also created the ravager to destroy. ¹⁷No weapon that is fashioned against you shall prosper, and you shall confute every tongue that rises against you in judgment. This is the heritage of the servants of the Lord and their vindication from me, says the Lord.*

Understanding the Word. Here, as again in the book of Revelation, when God wants to speak of the wonder and richness of a relationship with him, he resorts to speaking of a city adorned in precious jewels. Perhaps the stimulus for this is the language describing the temple, which we are told was decorated with precious jewels (1 Chron. 29:8; 2 Chron. 3:6). The people, who have felt abandoned and despised, defiled and dirty, are instead told that God will make them into his temple, his city, upon which he will lavish the rarest and most expensive adornments. Cast off? Hardly! Rejected? Never! In fact, Yahweh would all but bankrupt himself to show how precious his people are to him. Remember the larger context here. The people have said that God has forgotten them (49:14), that they are so defiled by their sin that God could never love them again (42:25). Yet God says here, and not for the first time, that they are precious to him and that he has removed every barrier between them. How has he done that? The answer is in 52:13–53:12. Yes, it would be hundreds of years before the cross would become a historical fact. But it was already a fact in the Godhead, and on the basis of its reality, there was, and is, no barrier to the lavish love of God flowing out to every one of us, his chosen.

In verse 13 the theme of children comes to the surface again, but here it is not the idea of their numbers that is emphasized. Here the emphasis is upon their teachability, as God himself teaches them. Isaiah 50:4–5 told us that this would be accomplished through the Servant, and John tells us that it is done by means of the Spirit (1 John 2:20, 27) whom Christ the Servant sent (John 14:26). Unlike their ancestors, who had proved unteachable, and were thus unsuccessful in their calling as God's people, these descendants (whom we may think of as the early Jewish Christians) did succeed in what God was calling them to become. (On "prosper" as "succeed," see the Week Eleven commentary.)

Verses 14–17 reiterate in several ways the truth that God's people are forever secure in him. Here, as is normal in the Old Testament, these promises are expressed in strictly physical and material terms. While there *is* unusual physical and material security for the individual and the nation that are living in accord with God's plans for life, it is important for us to recognize, as the New Testament makes plain, that in this fallen world, the only true security is spiritual. It is absolutely true, as this passage says, that the person who belongs wholly to God can weather the most severe attacks physically and materially and come through it the victor. We need only to think of some of the greatest hymn writers to see evidence of this. Isaac Watts, William Cowper, Fanny Crosby, Frances Havergal, George Matheson, and others were all people who suffered grievous physical and/or emotional distress. Yet they could all testify that "no weapon that is fashioned against you shall [succeed] . . . This is the heritage of the servants of [Yahweh]" (54:17).

1. Do you ever reflect on how precious you are to God? If not, why not?

2. Think of some people you know who have, by the grace of God, triumphed over various adversities in life. What was their secret?

3. Obviously, being taught by the Holy Spirit does not mean that we do not need other education. So what does being teachable in this way mean?

FOUR

The Covenant of David

Isaiah 55:1–5 *Ho, everyone who thirsts, come to the waters; and you that have no money, come, buy and eat! Come, buy wine and milk without money and without price. ²Why do you spend your money for that which is not bread, and your labor for that which does not satisfy? Listen carefully to me, and eat what is good, and delight yourselves in rich food. ³Incline your ear, and come to me; listen, so that you may live. I will make with you an everlasting covenant, my steadfast, sure love for David. ⁴See, I made him a witness to the peoples, a leader and commander for the peoples. ⁵See, you shall call nations that you do not know,* *and nations that do not know you shall run to you, because of the* LORD *your God, the Holy One of Israel, for he has glorified you.*

Understanding the Word. Here the invitation is made, if anything, even more emphatic than in the previous chapter. We sense the passion of God through the prophet. He grieves for those who thirst for some meaning in their lives, and for those who labor under a deep sense of divine disapproval. He mourns for those who spend their lives (the only real currency any of us have) trying desperately to satisfy their longings, quiet their fears, and fill the empty spaces in their souls. The Father, through Christ, by the Holy Spirit, has made provision for every need the human heart possesses. He has given us a full pardon for our sins; he has shown us what we are really longing for—a fulfilling relationship with him—and has made such a relationship fully available. He has promised strength for every trial, protection from every foe, and a joyous "welcome home" at the end of the journey. Yet, so many of his children turn up their noses at the rich banquet he has prepared because coming to it means we must admit that we are paupers, and are not even the rulers of our poverty. We would rather be sovereign in a pigpen than a servant in a palace. With Satan in Milton's *Paradise Lost* (1:261), we say, "Better to reign in Hell than serve in Heaven."

But what does God offer? He offers us a new covenant in place of the old one. The old one was the covenant of Moses. This one is the covenant of David. What is the difference between the two? Jeremiah 31:31–33 tells us. The old one was written on tablets of stone, that is, external to us, and as the apostle Paul tells us, was weak in that it could not defeat our inner self-centeredness (Rom. 7:14–16; 8:3), what Ezekiel call the heart of stone within us (Ezek. 36:26). But the new covenant, the covenant made possible through Jesus, the fulfillment of the promises to David, will be written on our hearts, hearts made soft and pliable by the grace of God. This new covenant is an expression of that unfailing love (*hesed*) that is absolutely dependable. It is that which sums up all that Yahweh is.

What will be the result of that new covenant working in the believer? Just as David was living evidence ("a witness") of what God can do in a person (and, tragically, what also happens when that person defies the grace of God), so those who are living in that new covenant will be witnesses (living evidence) of who God is, and as such, will draw people from around the world to Yahweh (see Isaiah 2:1–5; 43:8–13; 60:3).

1. Why do we humans prefer our way to God's way, even when we know it is leading us into trouble?

2. Does your manner of living make you attractive to others? Why or why not?

3. What in particular do you, as an individual, have to surrender in order to be in the covenant of David with God?

FIVE
Seek the Lord While He May Be Found

Isaiah 55:6–13 *Seek the L*ORD *while he may be found, call upon him while he is near;* [7]*let the wicked forsake their way, and the unrighteous their thoughts; let them return to the L*ORD*, that he may have mercy on them, and to our God, for he will abundantly pardon.* [8]*For my thoughts are not your thoughts, nor are your ways my ways, says the L*ORD*.* [9]*For as the heavens are higher than the earth, so are my ways higher than your ways and my thoughts than your thoughts.*

[10]*For as the rain and the snow come down from heaven, and do not return there until they have watered the earth, making it bring forth and sprout, giving seed to the sower and bread to the eater,* [11]*so shall my word be that goes out from my mouth; it shall not return to me empty, but it shall accomplish that which I purpose, and succeed in the thing for which I sent it.*

[12]*For you shall go out in joy, and be led back in peace; the mountains and the hills before you shall burst into song, and all the trees of the field shall clap their hands.* [13]*Instead of the thorn shall come up the cypress; instead of the brier shall come up the myrtle; and it shall be to the L*ORD *for a memorial, for an everlasting sign that shall not be cut off.*

Understanding the Word. Surely one of God's greatest gifts to us, and a mark of his deep respect for us, is the gift of rationality. Yahweh has not made us robots, programming us in advance with all we need to know. Rather, he has invited us to use our minds to discover the nature of the marvelous universe in which he has placed us. As the great Master-Teacher he delights in his students' discoveries. But like every good thing he has created, our rationality is capable of being perverted to evil. And as C. S. Lewis has the devil Screwtape say, the better the gift, the more capable of perversion. As a result, our rationality can lead us even to the denial of God himself. This is because while nothing about God is ever irrational, he is far beyond our rational comprehension: "The Light shines in the darkness, and the darkness did not comprehend it" (John 1:5 NASB). (The Greek word connotes surrounding something and containing it. Thus, some modern translations have, "has never extinguished it." But the idea that when we comprehend something, we contain it is quite relevant to the point here.)

So the admonition here is not to wait until we understand exactly how the Servant's self-sacrifice can make it possible for God to wipe the record of our sins clean and welcome us into his arms again. If we insist on God's explaining how he can do this in terms that our rationality can comprehend, we will wait until it is far too late. There is a bit of mystery here, but biography makes it very clear that conviction of sin and the sense that God is holding the door of heaven open for us do not last forever. Again and again we read of people who have rejected the invitation, especially in their early years, and have never really sensed it again. So if you have never actually invited Christ into your heart and you sense that he is asking to come in today, do not put off that great, "Yes!"

Since Christ's coming as the God-man, we today have a clearer understanding of how this great transaction was made possible, but if you were to look at any of the standard systematic theology books that have been written over the last millennium, you would see that there are almost as many theories of exactly how God reconciles us to himself through Christ ("atonement") as there are authors. In the end, it is still true that Yahweh's thoughts and ways are far beyond human rationality. He does not ask us to stop thinking, but he does call upon us to give up those ways and thoughts of ours that are wicked because they are self-serving (Isa. 55:7), and to embrace his ways and thoughts, which, although they are far beyond us (vv. 8–9), still guarantee to us that we can be restored to our Maker and can walk with him in untroubled fellowship (vv. 10–11).

When we do embrace those ways and thoughts, and God is permitted to have his way in our lives, then all creation rejoices (vv. 12–13), for in our restoration it sees the down payment on its own final restoration.

1. When we insist on making God capable of being apprehended by our rationality, what are we seeking to do?

2. Can you think of people you know who once sensed God calling them and put off a response, and now seem incapable of hearing the divine call?

3. Reflect on the way the apostle Peter's use of Isaiah 40:6–8 in 1 Peter 1:23–25 also relates to Isaiah 55:10–11.

COMMENTARY NOTES

A plain reading of Isaiah 54:9–10, 15–17 seems to say that Israel was absolutely secure in its land from the time of the return from exile (ca. 538 BC) until the end of time. There is no equivocation whatsoever in God's promises given in those verses. That being so, we must ask what happened in AD 135 and after. After the Jewish revolt in AD 70, the Jews were permitted to remain in the province of Judea (roughly equivalent to the ancient territory of Judah). But that was not the case with the revolt of Bar Kokhba that was finally put down in 135 BC. At that time the Romans made it a capital offense for a Jew to live in Judea. They also completely leveled Jerusalem and rebuilt it on the typical pattern of a Roman city. It was at this point that the worldwide Jewish dispersion really began to take hold.

How are we to explain this in view of the promises of Isaiah? Two possibilities present themselves. The first is that these promises are not given to the Israel of the exile, but to the Israel of the millennium, the thousand-year reign of Christ that will precede the final battle between Christ and evil (Rev. 20:1–6). In other words, it is only when Israel has accepted their Messiah (Rom. 11:26–33) that the full promises here and in Isaiah 60–62 will apply. Of course, not everyone believes that the passage in Revelation should be taken literally, but it remains one serious possibility.

The second possible explanation, and the one I think more likely, relates to the nature of prophetic revelation in the Old Testament. Unlike pagan thought, in which the future is predetermined and can be discerned through omens, the positions of the stars, and so on, biblical thought sees the future as being open and dependent upon continuing faithful human response to God. In other words, from God's perspective Israel is absolutely secure in his love. However, if they should reject that love, they would take themselves out from under that care, which is what they did when they rejected their Messiah, Jesus. This is the tragedy of Jewish history in the last two thousand years: none of it ever needed to happen.

Here's another point to consider: If, as I have maintained, and as the church has believed for the last two millennia, Jesus is the fulfillment of the prophecies regarding the Servant, we might ask what relevance those promises had for the returned exiles five hundred years before the coming of Christ. The answer to that question, I believe, is that the work Christ was going to accomplish on behalf of God's people in the future enabled him to take his people back into relationship with himself even before the fact. Had there been no such work to come, then the sins that had sent the people into exile would have remained an insuperable barrier to a renewed relationship with them.

Then, when Christ did actually come, the question for those alive at that time was whether they would recognize that this person was indeed the one who had been promised. If they did so, the loving relationship they had been enjoying over the previous centuries could then come to its full potential. If they did not recognize Christ, that did not mean that God was finished with his people Israel. But they have had to endure a great deal from the hand of God and will continue to do so until they finally come to that recognition, apparently at the end of time.

Now a question: What was the covenant with David that we see in 55:3, and what is its significance? In his covenant with Abraham, Yahweh made three promises: Abraham would receive a family, he would be given a land, and he would become a blessing to the nations. In his own lifetime Abraham received the first promise. He saw the birth of his son. But it was not until four hundred years later that his descendants, after having come out of Egypt, received the promise of the land. Up until that time there seems to have been a forward focus for the people. If they kept alive a memory of, and a certain devotion to, "the God of [their] ancestors" (Exod. 3:13), it was almost certainly because of that promise of the land to come, as Joseph, for one, expressed it (Gen. 50:24–25).

But it is apparent that after the tribes got into the land and received their allotments, they lost their forward focus. They no longer needed to keep faith with Yahweh because they thought they had

gotten all there was to get. This explains the downward spiral described in the book of Judges. By the time of Samuel, the situation was critical. How could God refocus their attention on the final, worldwide goal of the original promises? The answer lay in another covenant, the covenant with David. Although David was not immune from sinful failure, he was a man who was 100 percent for God. There was never any question where his loyalty lay. Thus when he wanted to build a house for God, God told him that a building was not what he wanted, but that he wanted to build a "house"—a family—for David (2 Sam. 7). It would be a "house" that would continue forever (even when any temple the Davidic dynasty might build for God was long gone) and would be the means whereby the beneficent reign of Yahweh would extend to the whole earth.

Would the royal dynasty be immune from judgment? Hardly! In fact, there would come a day when, humanly speaking, that royal dynasty would be destroyed. But would the "house" disappear? Never. This is the significance of the phrase "my steadfast, sure love for David" in 55:3. The Hebrew is "the completely dependable *heseds* of David." The point is that all God's unfailing, undeserved love as expressed to and through David is completely unchanging, and will be for all the world. The dynasty that had provided a forward look for Judah for 350 years might be gone, but the *hesed* of God expressed in that covenant with David was not gone, and the exiles could continue to look forward in the confidence that somehow, someway, God was still going to bless the world through them.

The tragedy, of course, was that their thoughts were not God's thoughts. They could only conceive of the Son of David as being a dominating, oppressive monarch who would put his enemies to death and would impose his "blessing" upon a subdued world. They could not conceive that the Servant and the Son of David could be one and the same, and that he would rule a kingdom where none would harm (11:9; 65:25) by means of his word.

WEEK TWELVE

GATHERING DISCUSSION OUTLINE

A. Open session in prayer.

B. View video for this week's readings.

C. What general impressions and thoughts do you have after considering the video and reading the daily writings on these scriptures?

D. Discuss questions selected from the daily readings.

> **1. KEY OBSERVATION:** God is the one who is the true supplier of our needs.
>
> **DISCUSSION QUESTION:** Where would you say the line is between our merely trying to supply our needs for ourselves, and trusting God to supply our needs?

> **2. KEY OBSERVATION:** God had expressed his compassion for us by becoming incarnate in Christ.
>
> **DISCUSSION QUESTION:** What are some specific ways in which the incarnation expresses God's compassion for us?

> **3. KEY OBSERVATION:** God's promises to bless us and make us secure do not mean that we will never suffer or face adversity.
>
> **DISCUSSION QUESTION:** Think of some people you know who have, by the grace of God, triumphed over various adversities in life. What was their secret?

4. **KEY OBSERVATION:** God invites us to stop trying to satisfy ourselves and our desires in our way, but to do it in his way.

   DISCUSSION QUESTION: Why do we humans prefer our way to God's way, even when we know it is leading us into trouble?

5. **KEY OBSERVATION:** God's ways and thoughts cannot be made subject to our rationality.

   DISCUSSION QUESTION: When we insist on making God capable of being apprehended by our rationality, what are we seeking to do?

E. What facts and information presented in the commentary portion of the lesson help you understand the weekly scripture?

F. Close session with prayer.